VISUAL QUICKSTART GUIDE

QUICKEN 2000

FOR WINDOWS

Tom Negrino

 Peachpit Press

Visual QuickStart Guide
Quicken 2000 for Windows
Tom Negrino

Peachpit Press
1249 Eighth Street
Berkeley, CA 94710
510/524-2178
800/283-9444
510/524-2221 fax

Find us on the World Wide Web at: http://www.peachpit.com

Peachpit Press is a division of Addison Wesley Longman

Copyright © 1999 Tom Negrino

Editor: Lisa Theobald
Production Coordinator: Mimi Heft
Cover design: The Visual Group
Compositor: David Van Ness
Indexer: Karin Arrigoni

ISBN 0-201-69965-6

0 9 8 7 6 5 4 3 2 1

Printed and bound in the United States of America

♻ Printed on recycled paper

Dedication

To my father, Joseph Negrino, who has touched so many people's lives, becoming more than their accountant; he's become their friend. Thanks for the inspiration, Dad.

Special Thanks to:

Tom Baer, for all of his work.

The folks at Peachpit:

My editor, Lisa Theobald, for shepherding the book through even when things got difficult.

Mimi Heft, for her production wizardry, and for taming Microsoft Word's templates.

Nancy Ruenzel and Marjorie Baer, for believing in the project.

The people at Intuit:

Kelly O'Neil, the lady with the answers.

Adam Samuels, for helping to get this book going.

I'd also like to thank my agent, StudioB's David Rogelberg.

Thanks once again to Sean Smith, for being the World's Best Kid™.

Last but never least, thanks always to Dori Smith, for her love, wisdom, and incredible support. I might be able to do this without you, but it wouldn't be nearly as much fun.

TABLE OF CONTENTS

TABLE OF CONTENTS

TABLE OF CONTENTS

INTRODUCTION

Money pervades our lives, simultaneously desired and disdained. Most of us can't get along without it and would love to have more of it. Yet despite its importance, many of us don't do an especially good job of managing the money that we do have. How often have you heard people say things like "I don't know where all my money goes"? Many people live from paycheck to paycheck, just floating along with no financial plan for the future and hardly any control over their financial present. In the meantime, they're building up consumer debt and digging themselves a hole that will take a long time to get out of.

Sound familiar? It certainly does to me; I was one of those people for many years. I finally got fed up with feeling that my finances were out of my control, so one December evening I bought a copy of Quicken Deluxe and promised myself that I would start using it when the new year began. I kept that promise, and melodramatic as it sounds, it changed my life. I used Quicken to take stock of my finances and identify where I was handling my money poorly. Then I came up with a plan to pay off my debts and start saving for the future. Today I'm happy to say that I no longer wonder what my financial picture is, because Quicken gives me all the information that I need.

If you want to get better control over your finances, this book is for you. I'll show you how to use Quicken to help you get out of debt, manage your present finances, and invest for the future.

Just the Facts, Ma'am

I have to admit that I don't have a lot of patience with computer books that are thick and heavy enough to cause injury if you accidentally drop them on your foot. I'd rather open a book, find out how to do a task, and toss the book back on the shelf without wading through endless blather and more details than I ever wanted to know.

In this book, I've organized different financial tasks into chapters, and within each chapter are step-by-step directions that tell you exactly how to accomplish various tasks.

On occasion, you'll see this icon:

It indicates that the feature being discussed pertains only to Quicken Deluxe 2000.

My Assumptions About You

In writing this book, I've made the following assumptions about you. First, you own one of the versions of Quicken 2000 and a Windows PC that's powerful enough to run the program. That's not a difficult requirement, as Quicken 2000 will run on machines using a 486 processor at 66 MHz (though a Pentium-class machine is recommended), with at least 16 MB of RAM, running Windows 95, Windows 98, or Windows NT 4.

I've also made the assumption that you're familiar with the basics of Windows. You don't need to be a Windows guru, although concepts such as selecting text, clicking and dragging, and using files and folders shouldn't stump you. If you need to brush up on the essentials, allow me to suggest that you pick up a copy of *Windows 98: Visual QuickStart Guide* by Steve Sagman, which coincidentally Peachpit Press also publishes.

Last, I've made the assumption that if you have bought this book, you're a person of uncommon discernment, style, and grace. If you're just leafing through these pages in a bookstore, I'm trusting you not to let me down.

What's Not in This Book

Because I wanted to write a book that was genuinely useful, rather than one that slavishly touched every base and documented every Quicken feature, I had to decide what I didn't want to put in the book. So I looked through Quicken for features that were little used or that weren't that great. The first feature to get the heave-ho was Budgeting. Making budgets is one of those things that everyone says they want to do, but hardly anyone really does. This isn't just my opinion; I've seen surveys of real Quicken users that bear me out. My apologies to you if you are one of the few, the proud, who really do budgets. A close relative to Budgeting is Forecasting, which also did not make the cut.

While I've included three chapters on investments, those chapters are intended for the relatively light-duty investor. If you have a modest stock portfolio, some mutual funds, and some other savings plans, the investment chapters should work just fine for you. But it you're constantly churning your portfolio, buying and selling options, and otherwise seriously playing the markets, you may find my investment chapters a bit thin. If that's the case, you'll find more detailed help in the Quicken User Guide and on Intuit's Web site, Quicken.com (`http://www.quicken.com`).

I've also skipped over some of Quicken's less interesting features, such as the Progress Bars (they work with Budgeting; check out the online help if you really need to know more about them) and the Quicken Home Inventory program—the latter is one of the few outright flops in the otherwise excellent Quicken package.

Let's Get Started

A popular bit of philosophy states that the journey is the reward. I'm afraid my pragmatic side says that when it comes to money, the reward is the reward. In this case, using Quicken can mean smarter control over your finances, and in turn a better and richer life for yourself and for your family. That's a journey well worth taking. Thanks for joining me.

Tom Negrino
August 1999

PART 1

GETTING
ORGANIZED

INTRODUCING QUICKEN 2000

1

Welcome to Quicken 2000! In this chapter, you'll learn how to install and start Quicken, convert old Quicken files (if you've been using an older version of the program), use Quicken's interface, ask Quicken for help, and customize the program so that it works the way you do.

Installing and Running Quicken for the First Time

Like most programs these days, Quicken provides step-by-step instructions for installation as soon as you load the product's CD-ROM. In case you need a little extra information, here's a bit of guidance to help you get the application up and running on your computer.

To install Quicken 2000:

1. Insert the Quicken 2000 CD-ROM into your CD-ROM drive. The CD will start up automatically and present a dialog box asking if you want to install Quicken (**Figure 1.1**). Click Yes.

2. Click Next in the Welcome screen of the Quicken Setup program (**Figure 1.2**).

3. The software license agreement appears. If you like reading this sort of thing, have at it. Most of us will just click Next.

4. In the Choose Destination Location window (**Figure 1.3**), choose where you want the Quicken folder to reside on your hard drive. By default, it's placed into a folder called QUICKENW at the root level of your main hard drive. If you want to put the folder somewhere else, click the Browse button and navigate to your desired location in the usual Windows fashion. When you have the folder where you want it, click Next.

Figure 1.1 To get started installing Quicken, click Yes.

Figure 1.2 The Quicken Setup Wizard walks you through installing the program.

Figure 1.3 You'll need to tell Setup where you want to install the Quicken folder.

Figure 1.4 Most people will choose the Express installation.

Figure 1.5 Both the Quicken program and QuickEntry have desktop shortcuts.

The Type of Installation window appears (**Figure 1.4**). Here you can choose the Express (full) installation or a Custom install. Express installs the components that most people will need for Quicken. This includes the Quicken program, Internet Explorer 5.00, and other common programs.

5. Choose Express unless you have a specific reason *not* to install some of these (for example, if you know you already have a later version of Internet Explorer installed). Then click Next.

6. In the confirmation window that appears, click the Start Copying button.

The Setup Complete window tells you that you need to restart your computer to complete the installation.

7. Click the Finish button to close the Setup program and restart your machine.

When you restart your computer, you'll see shortcuts for one or two Quicken-related programs on your desktop (**Figure 1.5**). One shortcut is for whichever version of Quicken you installed (Basic, Deluxe, or Home & Business) and the other (if you have anything but Quicken Basic) is for QuickEntry 2000.

INSTALLING AND RUNNING QUICKEN

To run Quicken 2000 for the first time:

1. Double-click the Quicken program shortcut on your desktop.

The Quicken program starts up, and the first of the Quicken New User Setup windows appears (**Figure 1.6**). This Setup Wizard will step you through creating your first account, your main checking account.

2. Click Next.

The next window (**Figure 1.7**) asks you to tell Quicken a bit of personal information.

3. Click the radio buttons that correspond to your situation, and then click Next.

4. In the next window (**Figure 1.8**), enter the name Quicken will use for your primary checking account into the Account Name field, and then enter the name of the bank if it does not appear on the pop-up menu. Then click Next.

5. Quicken asks if you have the last paper statement for this account (**Figure 1.9**). If you don't, click No and enter the opening balance for the account later. If you do have the statement, click Yes, and then click Next.

Figure 1.6 The New User Setup windows help you create your first checking account.

Figure 1.7 Quicken needs to know a little personal information to serve you better.

Figure 1.8 Enter a name and the location of your checking account.

Figure 1.9 Tell the program whether you have the last paper statement for the checking account.

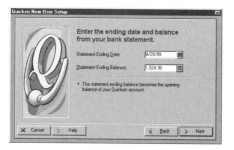

Figure 1.10 Enter the statement date and the ending balance for the account.

Figure 1.11 Check over your information to make sure it's correct, and then click Done.

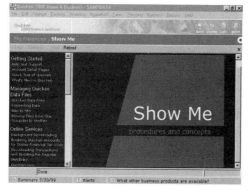

Figure 1.12 Review the introductory videos for some good starting information.

6. If you answered Yes to the question in step 5, Quicken opens the window shown in **Figure 1.10**. Enter the statement date and ending balance.

7. On the last setup window (**Figure 1.11**), review the information for accuracy and then click Done.

Quicken creates the checking account and opens the Quicken Show Me window (**Figure 1.12**) to show you the basics of in Quicken 2000. You'll see the multimedia video window on the right side of the screen.

8. Select a topic in the left frame and click the arrow at the bottom of the multimedia window to play the introductory video.

✔ Tips

- It's a good idea to take a look at all the initial multimedia help videos. It doesn't take a long time, and it will give you a good feel for the scope of Quicken 2000.

- Sometimes the Quicken Help window doesn't seem to notice that the Quicken CD-ROM is in the drive and won't show you the video file. To wake Help up, eject and reinsert the CD while the Help window is open.

What about my old Quicken files?

Good news! If you have an older version of Quicken on your hard drive, Quicken 2000 is smart enough to find and convert your old files to the current version's format without your needing to do a thing. The process is irreversible, but Quicken saves a backup copy of your old data file inside the Quicken folder.

Finding Your Way Around

Quicken has a lot of features, and the Quicken window is chock-full of gadgets to help you get around (**Figure 1.13**). Life is made a little easier by the Flyover Help feature that pops up little explanatory boxes when you pause the cursor over some of the buttons in the tool bar (**Figure 1.14**).

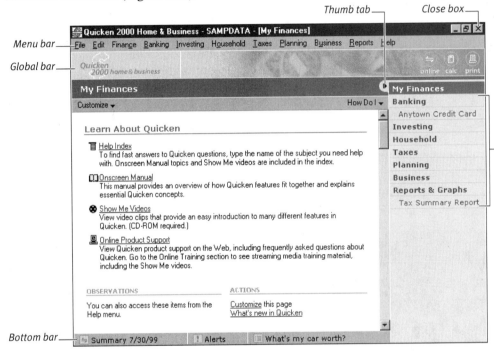

Figure 1.13 The Quicken window has a number of interface elements that make it easier for you to access the program's many features.

Figure 1.14 Resting the cursor over Transfer pops up "Record a transfer between Quicken accounts."

FINDING YOUR WAY AROUND

The menu bar

Along the top of the screen is the menu bar (**Figure 1.15**). As in any Windows program, the File, Edit, and Help menus hold most of the commands you'll need. It also contains much of what was included the activity bar in Quicken 99. Each menu in the bar covers a set of financial tasks.

◆ The **Finance** menu allows you to see overviews of your accounts, financial calendar, reminders, and alerts.

◆ The **Banking** menu commands affect different bank accounts, including checking, savings, and money-market accounts. You also issue commands for online banking from here.

◆ Use commands in the **Investing** menu to track stocks, bonds, mutual funds, 401(K)s, and other investments.

◆ Use the **Household** menu commands to deal with your net worth, loans, mortgages, and other assets.

◆ The **Taxes** menu includes commands that let categorize your transactions for tax purposes, identify possible tax deductions, and develop a strategy (a legal one, of course) to minimize your tax burden.

◆ The **Planning** menu offers commands that let you budget and forecast your finances and figure out how to get out of debt. Its calculators can help you plan for retirement and other goals.

◆ The **Reports** menu gives you access to a wide range of reports and graphs on many of your financial activities.

◆ The **Small Business** menu appears with the Home & Business version of Quicken only. Its commands allow you to create invoices, receive payments, and deal with business bills.

File Edit Finance Banking Investing Household Taxes Planning Business Reports Help

Figure 1.15 You can tell Quicken where to go and what to do from the menu bar.

FINDING YOUR WAY AROUND

The global bar

Below the menu bar is the global bar, a decorative banner with four buttons on the right: Online, Print, Calc, and Back.

- Clicking **Online** connects you to the Internet and a number of features, including online banking, financial data, insurance, and mortgage quotes.

- The **Print** button is a shortcut to sending items to the printer.

- Clicking **Calc** opens a desktop calculator that allows you to paste the result of a calculation in the appropriate place as you work in Quicken.

- Clicking the **Back** button takes you back to the previous screen.

The tool bar

Just below the title above the main Quicken window is the tool bar (**Figure 1.16**). As the content of the window changes, the tool bar offers an ever changing menu of options. When an "x" appears at the right side of the tool bar, you know that other windows are hiding under the window you're looking at. Clicking the "x" will return you to the previous screen, as will clicking the Back button in the global bar.

Open   Hide (x)   New   Edit   Delete   Options ▾   How Do I ▾   ✕

Figure 1.16 The tool bar changes to suit the frame below it.

Figure 1.17
QuickTabs make it easy to switch between open Quicken windows.

Figure 1.18 This dialog controls some features of the Quicken display.

QuickTabs

On the right side of the window, you'll see QuickTabs (**Figure 1.17**), which let you change between Quicken windows quickly and easily. Click a QuickTab to display a Financial Activity Center, which is also accessible from the menu bar.

To remove QuickTabs to free up space on your screen:

1. Choose Edit > Options > Quicken Program, and then click the QuickTabs tab (**Figure 1.18**).

2. Uncheck the Show QuickTabs box and click OK.

✔ Tip

■ To hide the QuickTabs, click the thumb tab with the arrow at the top of the QuickTab frame. To adjust the amount of space they occupy, move the cursor to the edge of their frame and, when it changes from the regular arrow to two vertical bars with arrows, drag it to the left or right.

FINDING YOUR WAY AROUND

11

The status bar

At the bottom of the window you'll see three buttons—Quicken Online, Alerts, and a button that changes in a seemingly random way to pose a number of questions designed to increase your anxiety, such as, "Am I paying too much for insurance?" and "Can I afford to pay for my child's education?" (**Figure 1.19**).

◆ Clicking **Quicken Online** connects you to Intuit's Web site and downloads a variety of information and software updates.

◆ Clicking **Alerts** opens the Set Up Alerts window, where you can tell Quicken to alert you about a number of events that are taking place or are about to occur.

◆ The **Question Box** sends you a set of screens designed to help answer a commonly asked question—and in some cases to sell you some service along the way.

| Quicken Online | Alerts | Can I afford to pay for my child's education? |

Figure 1.19 The Bottom Bar contains buttons for preset Alerts and Internet services.

Customizing Your Workspace

Quicken gives you a variety of ways to customize the program to suit your personal needs. While Quicken doesn't offer many options to customize the visual presentation of the workspace, the My Finances window that serves as the application's Home Page can be configured to include almost anything you need. You can even set up several variations and move easily among them.

Figure 1.20 Use Quicken's Help menu to get help fast.

Getting Onscreen Help

Quicken provides a number of options for onscreen help (although none are as wonderful as this book, naturally). Not surprisingly, you can get to the program's help files in the Help Topics window, via the Help menu (**Figure 1.20**). They are also accessible on the default My Finances page under "Learn About Quicken" (**Figure 1.21**). Some of the items on the menu aren't actually help—they're information or advertisements. Below, I list only the helpful stuff.

Index

Choose Index to see help keywords in the familiar Windows Help Topics window (**Figure 1.22**). Start typing a keyword to jump to it in the list. Then click Display to show the help screen.

Click the Contents tab to see the table of contents for the entire Help system. Here's where you access Quicken's Onscreen Manual (**Figure 1.23**).

Figure 1.21 Quicken's Home Page also offers a range of Help functions.

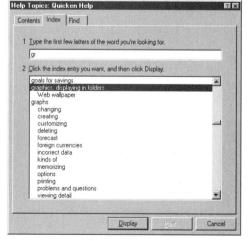

Figure 1.22 You can get to any entry in the Quicken Help Index just by typing the first few letters of the topic you want.

Figure 1.23 The same information is organized by topics when you choose Contents.

Current Window

Choose this option to open a standard Windows Help screen for the active window (**Figure 1.24**).

Show Me Videos

Choose Show Me Videos to return to the introductory videos displayed when you first installed Quicken 2000. Some are linked to the Internet.

Onscreen Manual

The Onscreen Manual is an overview of the Quicken program with a table of contents and a detailed index (**Figure 1.25**).

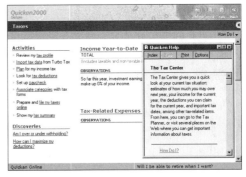

Figure 1.24 Selecting Current Window pops up a Help screen.

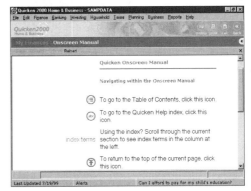

Figure 1.25 The Onscreen Manual is an overview of the Quicken program with a table of contents and a detailed index.

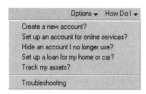

Figure 1.26 The How Do I menu offers a series of useful tips.

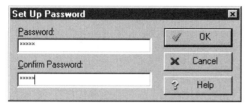

Figure 1.27 You can protect your data file from prying eyes with a password.

How Do I

At the right side of the scroll bar, you will find the words "How Do I" and an arrow. Click here to see a series of useful tips followed by "Get More Help" (**Figure 1.26**).

To quit Quicken:

◆ Choose File > Exit, or click the Close box (☒) in the upper-right corner of the window.

Quicken will close all open windows and return to the Windows desktop. You don't have to worry about saving your work because Quicken does it automatically.

To have Quicken remind you to back up your data file:

1. By default, Quicken reminds you to back up your data file after every third use of the program. To change that frequency, choose Edit > Options > Quicken program, and then click the General tab.

2. Change the number under "Backup after Running Quicken."

3. Click the OK button.

To protect your data file with a password:

1. Choose File > Passwords > File.

   The Set Up Password window appears (**Figure 1.27**).

2. Type a password.

3. Enter the password again to confirm.

4. Click the OK button.

✔ Tip

■ **Warning!** If you forget your password, the only way to access your data is to send the entire data file to Intuit. Its crack team of code breakers will remove your password. Intuit will also charge you a fee for the service.

SETTING UP ACCOUNTS

Quicken stores all your account information in a data file on your hard disk, which you create the first time you use the program. You need only one data file, but inside the data file you'll create a number of accounts. An account represents an *asset* (something that you own, such as the money in your checking account or some property) or a *liability* (a debt that you owe, such as the balance on your credit cards or a mortgage).

Quicken allows you to have as many or as few accounts as you wish (actually, the upper limit is 512 accounts per account type, but most people won't use more than a couple dozen accounts). Some people prefer to use Quicken to track only their main checking account, while other people create many accounts to track every penny.

In this chapter, you'll learn about the different account types within Quicken.

Using Accounts

Quicken has four kinds of accounts that you can use to track your assets:

- The **Bank** account tracks your checking accounts, savings accounts, money-market accounts, and debit cards. This is the only account type used to make electronic payments or to write checks.

- The **Asset** account tracks the value of an asset, such as real estate or your car.

- The **Investment** account tracks brokerage accounts that contain financial instruments, such as stocks and bonds.

- The **Cash** account is unlike the rest of the accounts because no corresponding account exists in a financial institution. You use the Cash account to track out-of-pocket expenses. For example, let's say that you withdraw $100 from an ATM. In Quicken, that amount comes out of your checking account and goes into the Cash account. As you spend the money, you can make notations in the Cash account to track where that money has gone.

Quicken also has two account types to track your liabilities:

- **Credit Card** accounts track your credit cards, equity lines, and other lines of credit.

- **Liability** accounts are usually loans, such as a mortgage or car loan.

If you're using Quicken Home & Business, you'll see two other kinds of accounts:

- The **Invoice/Receivables** account tracks customer invoices and other amounts people owe your business.

- The **Bills/Payables** account takes care of bills to vendors and how much your business owes.

Figure 2.1 The Create New Account window shows all the possible Quicken account types.

Figure 2.2 The first of the EasyStep windows for creating an account always asks you to name the new account.

Figure 2.3 Let Quicken know if you have the last paper statement for this account.

To create a new account with EasyStep:

1. Choose Banking > Banking Activities > Create New Account.

   or

   From the Account List, click New in the tool bar.

   or

   From the Banking Center's list of Activities, choose Create a New Account.

   The Create New Account window (**Figure 2.1**) appears.

2. Select the radio button corresponding to the kind of account you wish to create. Click Next.

   You'll see a setup window for the kind of account you selected. In the example shown, I picked Credit Card as the type, so I went to Credit Card Account Setup (**Figure 2.2**).

3. Enter the name of the account and the optional description, and then click Next.

4. Quicken next asks if you have the last statement for the account (**Figure 2.3**). If you have the statement, click Yes; if you don't, you can enter the opening balance later in the account's register. Click Next.

   (continued)

5. Enter an opening balance, and, if necessary, change the date (**Figure 2.4**). See **Table 2.1** for guidance on which amounts and dates to use for opening balances. Click Next.

6. The next window asks if the account is set up for online access (this screen may not show up for some account types because it won't apply). Answer Yes or No, and then click Next.

7. For credit card accounts, you can enter the credit limit. If you do, Quicken will show your remaining credit in the account register. Click Next.

8. The Summary window (**Figure 2.5**) contains all of the information you just entered. Review it, and click Done to create the account. Quicken then opens the register for the new account so that you can start making entries.

✔ Tip

■ You don't have to go through each EasyStep window; it's faster to create new accounts by following steps 1 through 3, jumping to the Summary window by clicking the Summary tab in the Account Setup window, then entering all of the information in the Summary window.

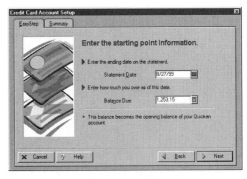

Figure 2.4 You'll need to tell Quicken the opening balance and the date you want to start tracking the account.

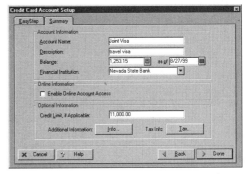

Figure 2.5 You can use the Summary window for review or initial entry of the account information.

Table 2.1

Entering Opening Balances

ACCOUNT TYPE	OPENING BALANCE	DATE
Bank	New balance from your last bank statement	Date of your last statement
Credit card	New balance from your last statement	Date of your last statement
Asset	The asset's current value	Today's date
Liability	The liability's current value	Today's date
Investment	See Chapter 14	
Cash	Current cash on hand	Today's date

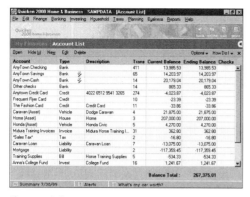

Figure 2.6 The Account List lets you see all of your accounts.

To edit an account:

1. Choose Finance > Account List or press Ctrl A. The Account List window appears (**Figure 2.6**).

2. Select an account and click the Edit button in the tool bar. An attributes and status window for the selected account appears.

3. Change the account information, and then click the Done button.

To delete an account:

1. Choose Finance > Account List or press Ctrl A.

   The Account List appears.

2. Select an account, and then click the Delete button. This process is irreversible, and you'll need to type *yes* in the deletion confirmation dialog. Then click the OK button (**Figure 2.7**).

✔ Tips

- You'll hardly ever need to delete an account. When you do, you lose the record of all the transactions that ever occurred in that account. Because this can mess up your reports, you're usually better off hiding an account.

- If you no longer use an account and you don't want it cluttering up your Accounts window, select it and click the Hide button on the tool bar. To see the account again, choose View Hidden Accounts from the Options pop-up menu. The account can be returned to normal status by clicking again on the Hide button.

Figure 2.7 Deleting an account gets rid of all of its associated transactions, so you have to type *yes* to make sure that you don't delete an account by mistake.

TRACKING WITH CATEGORIES

3

The point of using Quicken is to gain better control over your finances. To achieve that control, you need to know where your money comes from and where it goes. You use Quicken's *categories* to track the flow of money. A category is simply a label that you assign to a transaction. For example, when you buy food at the grocery store and record the transaction in a Quicken register, you can record it under the Groceries category. Later, when you're curious about how much money you spend on groceries, you can create a report that adds up all of your transactions for groceries.

By categorizing all of your transactions in Quicken, you can generate reports about the details of your income and expenses, save time and money while preparing your tax returns, and even set up budgets and compare what you're actually spending to what you had planned to spend.

Assigning Categories

Because you use categories to track the flow of money, you are naturally concerned about whether the money is flowing in or out. You track money that is flowing in, such as your paycheck and investment income, using income categories. And you track money that you spend on your mortgage, utilities, groceries, entertainment, and other bills using expense categories.

You can—and should—assign a category to each transaction that you enter into Quicken. You should also use the same category names consistently throughout your Quicken accounts. For example, if you go to the doctor and pay with a check, you would enter that check under the Medical category in your checking account register. If on a subsequent visit you pay with a credit card, you would enter the transaction in your credit card account register using the Medical category. This consistency is important: Consistent information leads to accurate reports.

When you created your data file (see Chapter 1), you probably included one of the preset categories lists, either the home categories or the business categories. You can use these category lists as is, but most people customize their categories to better reflect their particular financial situations.

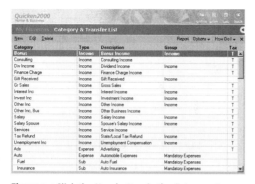

Figure 3.1 Click the New button in the Category & Transfer List window to create a new category.

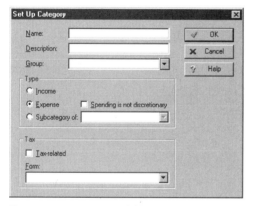

Figure 3.2 Enter a name and description in the Set Up Category dialog box.

Assigning Subcategories

You'll often want to track several types of income or expenses that are related to a single category. Quicken allows you to use subcategories to handle these relationships. For example, under the Medical category, you might have separate subcategories for Doctors, Dentists, Prescriptions, and Insurance. Later, when you run an expense report, you'll be able to see just how much money you've spent on each of the Medical subcategories.

To create a new category or subcategory:

1. Choose Finance > Category & Transfer List. The Category & Transfer List appears (**Figure 3.1**).

2. At the top of the Category & Transfer List window, click the New button. The Set Up Category dialog box appears (**Figure 3.2**).

3. Enter a name for the category in the Name field.

4. Enter a description for the category in the Description field (this is optional).

5. If you want to assign the category to a group (*groups* allow you to gather together related income or expenses for easier reporting), click the drop-down arrow and select the group name you want from the list (optional).

6. Select the appropriate radio button for the new category type (Income, Expense, or Subcategory of).

(continued)

ASSIGNING SUBCATEGORIES

7. If you want this category to be a subcategory of an existing category, click the
Subcategory of radio button, and then
click the drop-down arrow to see a list of
existing categories. Select the category
that you want to be the parent category
of your new subcategory.

8. Click the Tax-related check box if you
want to use the category to track tax-
related income or expenses. Then click
the down arrow of the drop-down list
to select the appropriate tax form
(**Figure 3.3**). See "Using Tax Links" later
in this chapter.

9. Click the OK button. Quicken creates the
category and adds it to the list in the
Category & Transfer List window.

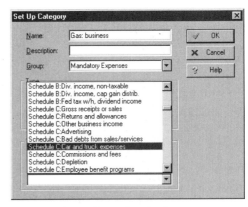

Figure 3.3 Choose the tax form for the category or
subcategory from this drop-down list.

To edit or delete a category or subcategory:

1. Select the category or subcategory in the Category & Transfer List window.

2. Click the Edit button. The Edit Category dialog box appears—which works in the same way as the Set Up Category dialog box. Make your changes, and then click the Change button.

    or

    Click the Delete button. When Quicken asks you to confirm the deletion, click Yes.

How Detailed Should I Get?

Quicken's preset categories are useful, but they're unlikely to completely satisfy your needs. No problem—just add more categories. But how many are enough?

The answer depends on the complexity of your financial picture and the level of detail you want in tracking it. Here's an example. Robert is in sales and is constantly on the road. The company reimburses Robert for some of his auto expenses, so he tracks those expenses in great detail. Under his main Auto category, he has included subcategories for Maintenance, Fuel, Insurance, and so on. Robert creates monthly Auto expense reports so that he can be reimbursed.

Susan works as an executive for the same corporation. She's curious to know how much she spends each year on her car. She doesn't care about the details; she just wants to know if her car expenses are growing or shrinking from year to year. So she uses one Auto category to track all expenses related to her car.

Your answer to the above question, then, depends on what kind of information is important to you. In general, you'll want to create subcategories for important elements so that you can track income and expenses in detail.

ASSIGNING SUBCATEGORIES

Using Tax Links

Quicken makes it easy for you to create tax reports by marking a selected category as tax-related and then assigning that category to a line item from a particular tax form. Several of the preset categories are already assigned to tax forms; these are marked with a T in the Tax column in the Category & Transfer List window.

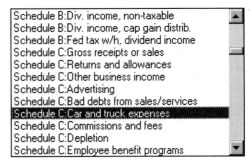

Figure 3.4 Scroll through the Form list and select the appropriate item.

To assign a tax link:

1. Select a category or subcategory in the Category & Transfer List window.

2. Click the Edit button. The Edit Category dialog box appears.

3. Click the Tax-related check box, and then scroll through the Form list and select the appropriate item (**Figure 3.4**).

4. Click the OK button. Quicken links that line item to the category you selected in step 1.

Using Classes

You can also group transactions by using *classes*. Classes do not replace categories; instead, a class adds an extra level to a transaction that you've already assigned to a category. When you assign a category to a transaction, you can also assign a class to the transaction by appending a slash (/), followed by the class name, to the category name. For example, Bob's medical expenses could be categorized as Medical/Bob.

You can use classes to avoid creating unnecessary subcategories. In the example above, it's possible (although probably inefficient) to add a Bob subcategory, another for Lisa, and so on for the entire family, all under the Medical category. The trouble with doing this is that you would need to create these subcategories for every category you could assign to a different family member. Pretty soon, you'd have about a zillion categories and subcategories. Instead, it's probably better to create a class for each family member and then assign that class to transactions as necessary.

Unlike categories, preset classes don't come with Quicken; you'll have to create and define your own. But like subcategories, subclasses are easy to create.

To create a class or subclass:

1. Choose Lists > Class, or press Ctrl L. The Class List window appears (**Figure 3.5**).

2. Click the New button. The Set Up Class dialog box appears (**Figure 3.6**).

3. Enter the name and (optionally) a description of the class, and then click the OK button. The name of the new class appears in the Class List window.

To edit or delete a class:

1. Select the class in the Class List window.

2. Click the Edit button. The Edit Class dialog box appears—this works in the same way as the Set Up Class dialog box. Make your changes, and then click the Change button.

    or

    Click the Delete button. When Quicken asks you to confirm the deletion, click Yes.

✔ Tips

■ Classes are a great way to help you differentiate personal and business expenses. For example, you can create a class called Business and assign it to categories that you also use for personal expenses. (For example, you can classify some meals as Dining/Business.)

■ If you have many clients, you can use classes to track income expenses separately for each client. In the same way, you can create classes for projects or particular jobs.

■ You can't change a class into a category or vice versa.

■ If you rename a class, category, subclass, or subcategory, Quicken replaces the old name with the new one in all transactions that contained the old name.

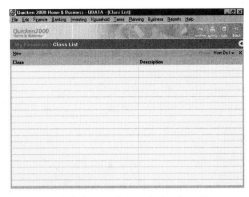

Figure 3.5 Click the New button in the Class List window to create a new class.

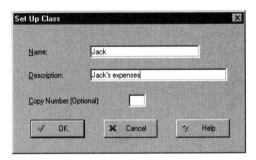

Figure 3.6 Enter a name and description for the new class in the Set Up Class dialog box.

USING THE
ACCOUNT REGISTERS

4

A *transaction* can be anything that changes the balance of an account. For a checking account, it could be writing a check, making a deposit, or withdrawing cash from the ATM. For a credit card account, it could be making a payment or a purchase. And for a stock portfolio account, transactions include buying shares and reinvesting dividends.

Every account in Quicken has an *account register* in which you enter transactions. Quicken's registers look and act much like paper checkbook registers, which makes them familiar and easy to use. One nice difference from paper, however, is that a Quicken register does the math for you and keeps a running balance automatically.

In this chapter, you'll learn how to enter transactions in the account registers, how to enter your paycheck information into Quicken, how to use Quicken to keep track of your credit cards, and how to use Quicken's data entry aids to save you typing and time.

Entering Checking Account Transactions

Checks, deposits, and transfers are all transactions that need to be entered in your account register. In boxes called *fields*, Quicken's checking account register (**Figure 4.1**) contains all the information you need about a transaction, including date, check number, payee, and transaction amount. In addition, Quicken provides category and memo fields along with check boxes to indicate reimbursable expenses and whether the transaction has cleared your bank. Finally, a running balance column does the math for you; Quicken won't let you make changes in this column.

You can enter checks that you intend to print from within Quicken in either the register or the Write Checks window. (See Chapter 6 for more about printing checks.)

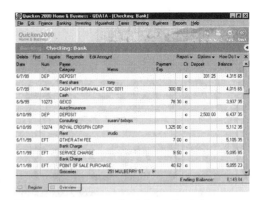

Figure 4.1 Enter transaction information in boxes called fields in the account register.

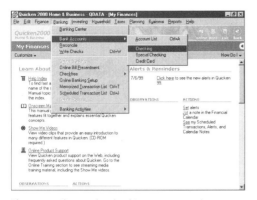

Figure 4.2 Choose the checking account register you want from the hierarchical menus.

Figure 4.3 A fresh line appears in the register, ready for you to fill it in.

Figure 4.4 Click the calendar icon to change the date.

To enter a check or a deposit:

1. Choose Banking > Bank Accounts (**Figure 4.2**), and then choose the account you want to use from the list, or press Ctrl R to open the last register you had open. If the account is open but not on top of your desktop, you can choose it from QuickTabs. (See Chapter 1 for more on QuickTabs.)

   A new line in the account register appears with the Date field highlighted and the current date filled in (**Figure 4.3**).

2. You can change the date by typing in a new date, clicking the calendar icon next to the date (**Figure 4.4**), or using the date keyboard shortcuts shown in **Table 4.1**.

   (continued)

Table 4.1

Keyboard shortcuts for the Date field	
SHORTCUT	WHAT IT DOES
+	Next day
–	Previous day
t	Today
m	Beginning of the current month
h	End of the current month
y	Beginning of the current year
r	End of the current year

3. Press the [Tab] key to move to the Num (for Number) field. If you're writing a check, enter the check number in the Number field. (To have Quicken automatically enter the next number in your check sequence, press the plus ([+]) key). If you're entering another kind of transaction, choose that transaction type from the pop-up menu in the Number field (**Figure 4.5**). See **Table 4.2** for the keyboard shortcuts you can use for transaction types.

4. Press the [Tab] key to move to the next field, Payee, and enter the name of the payee (for a check) or a description (for a deposit or transfer).

5. Press [Tab] to enter the payment or deposit amount in the appropriate field.

6. Click the Category field, under the Payee field. Assign a category to the transaction by typing it into the Category field.

The QuickFill feature fills in the category name from the pop-up menu (**Figure 4.6**) after you enter the first few letters. (See Chapter 5 for more information about QuickFill.) You can also use the pop-up menu in the Category field to select the category.

7. If you want to add a class to the category, type a slash ([/]) at the end of the category name, and then type the class name (optional).

8. Enter a memo about the transaction and, if appropriate, mark it as a reimbursable expense by clicking the Exp field.

9. Click the Enter button (or press the [Enter] key on the keyboard).

Quicken saves the transaction, adds it to the register, and updates the running account balance.

Figure 4.5 Choose a transaction type from the pop-up menu in the Number field.

Figure 4.6 The QuickFill pop-up menu lets you easily choose a category for your entry.

Table 4.2

Keyboard shortcuts for the Number field	
SHORTCUT	WHAT IT DOES
+	Enters the next check number
−	Subtracts a check number
a	ATM, an ATM transaction
d	DEP, a deposit
e	EFT, Electronic Funds Transfer
p	PRINT, a check to be printed
s	SEND, an electronic payment to be sent
t	TXFR, a transfer to another Quicken account

✔ Tips

■ Some people prefer to use the (Enter) key instead of the (Tab) key to move from field to field. To change Quicken's behavior, choose Edit > Options > Register and then click the QuickFill tab of the window. Click the check box labeled "Use Enter Key to Move Between Fields."

■ You can add to the transaction types available in the Num field by opening the pop-up menu and selecting Edit List.

■ If you need to write a postdated check, enter a future date in the Date field. At the bottom of the register, Quicken will display Balance Today and Ending Balance, showing the balance as of the day of the postdated check.

■ To enter a date quickly in the current month, type just the date and Quicken will fill in the rest when you tab to the next field.

■ Enter ATM withdrawals quickly by using QuickFill and starting your description with a number. For example, if you regularly withdraw $80, use the description 80 ATM. The next time you record an ATM withdrawal, simply type *80* in the Payee field and Quicken will complete the entry.

■ In any field for which QuickFill works, you can use the up and down arrow keys to scroll alphabetically through the possible matches. For example, if you type *Hom* in the Description field, QuickFill might guess "Home Depot." Pressing the down arrow key would tell QuickFill to try the next possibility in the QuickFill list, "Home Savings." Pressing the up arrow key scrolls backward alphabetically.

Splitting Transactions

Many transactions need to be divided among multiple categories. This is referred to as *splitting* the transaction. For example, at a service station you might write a single check that covers both gasoline and auto repairs. When you enter that transaction, you will enter a category name and amount for each part of the split. You can split checks that you write or payments that you receive. You can also record deposits consisting of a number of checks as splits.

To split a transaction:

1. Open a checking account register.

2. Enter the date, check number, payee, and payment or deposit amount.

3. Click the Split button in the register. The Split Transaction Window appears (**Figure 4.7**).

4. Enter a category for the first Category field, either by typing it in or by choosing it from the pop-up menu.

5. Type a memo in the first Memo field (optional).

6. Type the amount you want to allocate to the first category in the first Amount field.

   Quicken subtracts that amount from the total and puts the remainder in the next Amount field.

7. Enter the next category and amount on the next line. Repeat this until you have allocated the entire payment or deposit amount.

   You can add as many lines of categories as you need to a split transaction.

8. Click the OK button to save the transaction, properly allocated to multiple categories.

Figure 4.7 Use the Split Transaction Window to enter separate payment categories in the register.

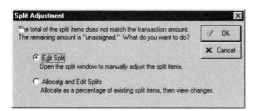

Figure 4.8 If you adjust an amount entered as a split without adjusting the details, Quicken will politely remind you, and ask what you want to do to correct the problem.

✔ Tips

- If you decide that you don't want to split the transaction, click the Cancel button in the Split Transaction Window to delete all the information in the split lines.

- If you want to split amounts but don't want to figure the total amount by adding up the split amounts yourself, Quicken can add up the total for you. For example, if you make one deposit that includes several checks from different categories, enter the amounts in all the split lines. As you add information, Quicken updates the total amount in the Deposit field.

- If you change the amount of a deposit or payment that you have already entered as a split, the difference will appear as a remainder that you will need to assign to one of your existing categories or to a new one.

- If the total of the split items does not match the total transaction amount, Quicken will ask you what you want to do with the "unassigned" amount in the Split Adjustment dialog box (**Figure 4.8**).

Entering Paychecks

You can enter paychecks as a split transaction, but doing so is a bit different than entering other transactions. Because paychecks are subject to payroll deductions, you need to show the gross amount and the deductions in the split lines.

To enter a paycheck:

1. Open a checking account register.

2. Enter the date, press the ⒟ key to add DEP to the Number field, enter a description, and then enter the net amount of your paycheck in the Deposit field.

   The net amount is your salary, minus all the deductions: the amount of the paycheck.

3. Click the Split button to open the Split Transaction Window.

4. In the first Category field, enter *Salary*.

5. Enter a memo in the Memo field (optional).

6. Enter the gross amount of your salary in the first Amount field.

7. In the next Category field, enter the first category for your deductions. For example, you might want to use *Taxes:Fed* as the category.

Figure 4.9 Enter your deductions as negative amounts so they will be subtracted from the gross amount.

8. In this and all subsequent split lines, enter your deductions as negative amounts so they will be subtracted from the gross (**Figure 4.9**). Continue to add lines until all your deductions are allocated.

9. Click the OK button when you're done.

✔ Tip

■ People's paycheck amounts usually don't change very often. You can save a lot of repetitive data entry by having Quicken memorize the transaction. Simply select the transaction and choose Edit > Transaction > Memorize, or press Ctrl M. Note that you probably won't want to memorize the amount information as percentages, since any variations from check to check are not likely to be evenly distributed across all the categories.

Using Paycheck Setup

The previous section showed you how to set up your paycheck manually, using a split transaction. But Quicken also has a Paycheck Wizard to help you through the process. You need to enter your paycheck this way only once, and Quicken will remember it for you for every subsequent paycheck.

To set up your paycheck using the Paycheck Wizard:

1. Choose Banking > Banking Activities > Set up my Paycheck as a register transaction.

   or

   Choose Taxes > Tax Activities > Set up my Paycheck.

   The Welcome tab of the Paycheck Setup window appears (**Figure 4.10**).

2. Read the information on the Welcome tab, and then click the Next button.

   The first of the EasyStep windows appears (**Figure 4.11**). Quicken will automatically create deduction entries for federal, state, Social Security, Medicare taxes, and disability insurance.

3. If you have additional, optional paycheck deductions made, such as 401(K) deductions, check them in this window.

4. Click the Next button. When the next EasyStep window appears (**Figure 4.12**), enter the name of the paycheck as you want it to appear in the register and then pick the frequency of the check from the drop-down list.

Figure 4.10 The Welcome tab of the Paycheck Setup Wizard.

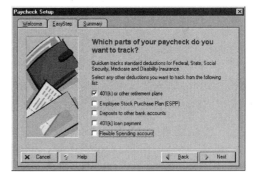

Figure 4.11 You can record additional deductions in this window.

Figure 4.12 Enter a name and the frequency of the paycheck here.

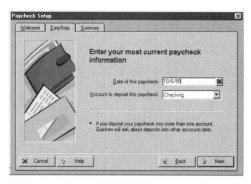

Figure 4.13 The next check date and which Quicken account to use goes here.

Figure 4.14 Enter the gross and net paycheck amounts in this window.

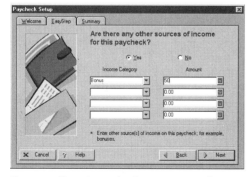

Figure 4.15 If you have other income sources that appear on the check, add them in this window.

5. In the next EasyStep window (**Figure 4.13**),enter the date of your most recent paycheck, and then choose the account into which you want to deposit it. Click the Next button.

6. Enter the gross and net amounts of your paycheck. Then choose an income category—you'll usually choose the Salary category (**Figure 4.14**).

7. Click the Next button to open a window that allows you to enter any other income sources for this paycheck (**Figure 4.15**). Enter an additional income category and amount for this paycheck (bonus income, for example).

(continued)

8. Click the Next button to open the standard tax deductions window (**Figure 4.16**). Enter the amounts withheld from your salary for each of the applicable standard categories: federal taxes, state taxes, Social Security (FICA) taxes, Medicare taxes, and State Disability Insurance (SDI).

9. Click the Next button to display the additional taxes window (**Figure 4.17**). If additional taxes are deducted from your paycheck, click the Yes radio button and enter the tax category and amount.

10. Click the Next button, and Quicken opens windows for each of the voluntary deductions you have chosen in step 2. If 401(K) or other retirement deductions are made to your paycheck, enter the name of the Quicken retirement account and the amount of your contribution (**Figure 4.18**). If your paycheck includes the employer's matching contribution, subtract it and enter only your contribution here.

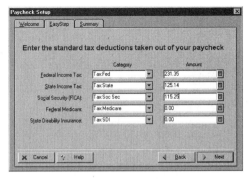

Figure 4.16 Itemize the usually painful taxes that are deducted from your check here.

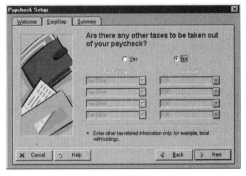

Figure 4.17 If you have additional taxes taken out, you'll enter them in this window.

Figure 4.18 Enter retirement deductions on this screen.

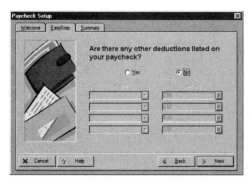

Figure 4.19 If any miscellaneous deductions get taken out of your check, enter them in this screen.

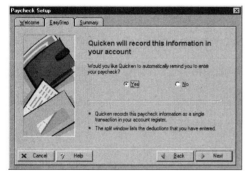

Figure 4.20 You can choose whether or not to have Quicken remind you to enter your paycheck.

Figure 4.21 Review your entries in the Summary screen—then you're done setting up your paycheck.

11. Click the Next button to open the miscellaneous deductions window (**Figure 4.19**). If any additional deductions apply, click the Yes radio button and add the appropriate categories and amounts.

12. Click Next to open the reminder window (**Figure 4.20**). If you want Quicken to remind you automatically to enter your paycheck (and that's why you've been using this Wizard, after all), click the Yes button.

13. Finally, click the Next button to open the Summary window (**Figure 4.21**). Review your entries. If you want to change anything, you can click on an amount or memo field to change it. Click the Done button to record the transaction.

Entering Credit Card Charges

Entering transactions in a credit card register is a lot like entering transactions in a bank account register. In the credit card register, however, the headings Charge and Payment appear rather than Payment and Deposit (**Figure 4.22**). (Another difference, of course, is that in a credit card register, you prefer a zero balance, a number most people wouldn't want to see as the balance for their checking account.)

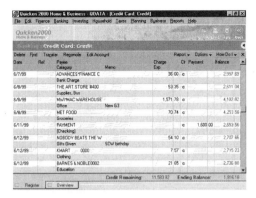

Figure 4.22 Enter information in the Charge and Payment fields in the credit card register.

To enter credit card charges:

1. Choose Banking > Bank Accounts to open the register for your credit card.

2. Enter the date of the credit card transaction.

   Notice that instead of the Check number field, the credit card register includes a Reference number field. Using this field is optional.

3. Enter the payee and the amount of the charge.

4. Enter the category.

5. Enter a memo about the charge (optional).

6. Click the Record button.

✔ Tips

- Don't forget to enter finance charges. You can do that here, or when you reconcile the account (see Chapter 9).

- You can dramatically reduce the amount of data entry in credit card accounts by setting up the account for online banking, which lets you download all the transactions from the bank to the account register. See Chapter 10 for more information about online banking.

Transfer categories

Figure 4.23 You can view the transfer categories in your data file by scrolling to the bottom of the Category & Transfer List.

Transferring Money Between Accounts

Because you often need to transfer money between accounts, Quicken gives you a streamlined way to do it. For example, when you write a check or transfer money electronically from your checking account to make a payment to your credit card account, money flows out of the checking account and into the credit card account, decreasing the credit card's balance. Quicken makes it easy to update both accounts so you don't have to enter the same transaction in both registers. To accomplish this, Quicken uses special *transfer categories* that refer to other Quicken accounts. You can view the transfer categories in your data file by choosing Finance > Category & Transfer and scrolling to the bottom of the window (**Figure 4.23**). The categories enclosed in square brackets are the transfer categories.

In the first example below, you'll see how to use transfer categories to transfer money from your checking account to your savings account. The next example shows you how to transfer money between accounts using the Transfer command.

To transfer money from one account to another:

1. Open a checking account register.

2. Enter the date in a new transaction.

3. In the Number field, press the ⊤ key. Quicken will add TXFR to the Number field to signify that this is a transfer.

4. Enter a description of the transfer in the Payee field.

5. In this example, money is moving from checking to make a payment on your credit card, so enter an amount in the Payment field. (If the money were flowing from savings to checking, you would add the amount to the Deposit field.)

6. In the Category field, press the left bracket (⟦) key, and then start to type the name of the destination account.

   or

   Choose the credit card account from the pop-up menu in the Category field. Your register should look something like **Figure 4.24.**

7. Click the Enter button. Quicken saves the transaction in the checking account register and creates a parallel transaction in the credit card account register.

Figure 4.24 Click the Enter button and Quicken saves the transaction.

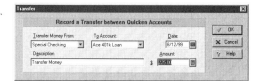

Figure 4.25 A transaction entered with the Transfer dialog is recorded simultaneously into two account registers.

To use the Transfer command:

1. At the top of the register, click the Transfer button. The Record a Transfer between Quicken Accounts window appears (**Figure 4.25**).

2. Using the Transfer Money From drop-down list, choose the source account for the transfer.

3. Using the To Account drop-down list, choose the destination account for the transfer.

4. Enter the date, a description (Transfer Money appears here by default), and the amount you want to transfer.

5. Click the OK button.

   Quicken creates a transaction in both the source and destination accounts.

Changing Transactions

Unlike some other financial programs, Quicken allows you to make changes to transactions at any time. You can edit, delete, or void transactions whenever necessary.

To edit a transaction:

1. Open the account register that contains the transaction you want to edit.

2. Click on a transaction to select it.

3. In any field of the transaction, select the incorrect information and type over it to replace it.

4. Click the Record button in the account register.

To delete a transaction:

1. Open the account register that contains the transaction you want to delete.

2. Click on a transaction to select it.

3. Choose Edit > Transaction > Delete, or press Ctrl D, or click the Delete button at the top of the register window. Quicken will ask you to confirm the deletion (**Figure 4.26**).

4. Click the Yes button. Quicken deletes the transaction.

To void a transaction:

1. Open the account register that contains the transaction you want to void.

2. Click on a transaction to select it.

3. Choose Edit > Transaction > Void. Quicken removes the amount in the Payment or Deposit field and adds **VOID** at the beginning of the Payee field.

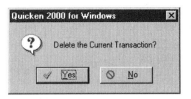

Figure 4.26 Click Yes to confirm the transaction deletion.

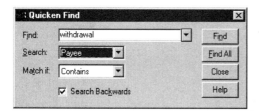

Figure 4.27 Enter the text that you wish to search for in the Find field.

Finding Transactions

You can search through account registers to find a particular transaction. This feature is most useful when you're entering a transaction and wish to be reminded of the details of a previous transaction.

Quicken will also let you find a group of transactions, as discussed below. Quicken is a very powerful tool for creating all manner of very specific and quite sophisticated reports, but we'll go into that later in the book.

To find a transaction:

1. Open the account register in which you want to find a transaction.

2. Choose Edit > Find & Replace > Find, select Find from the top of the register, or press Ctrl F.
   The Find dialog box appears (**Figure 4.27**).

3. In the Find field, enter the text that you wish to search for. Make choices from the Search and Match if pop-up menus to narrow your search.

4. Click the Find button to find the next occurrence of your search text.

5. When you're done with your search, click the Close box in the Find window.

To find a group of transactions:

1. You can select Find All in the Find dialog to see a list of the occurrences of your target in all your accounts (**Figure 4.28**).

   or

   Double-click on any item to be instantly transported there.

2. Clicking Back in the Banner bar will return you to the list where you can choose another.

Or

◆ Click Report in the tool bar to see either all the instances (in this register) of Amounts spent in this category or Payments made to this payee (**Figure 4.29**).

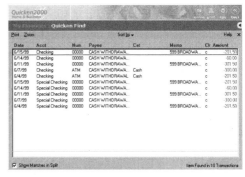

Figure 4.28 When you choose Find All, you get a list of all occurrences.

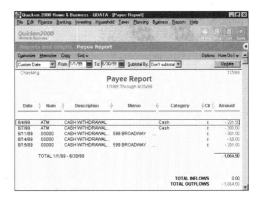

Figure 4.29 A Payee report shows where the term appears in one register.

Figure 4.30 The QuickEntry shortcut opens the QuickEntry program, which lets you enter transactions fast without opening the main program.

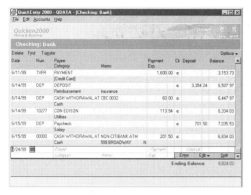

Figure 4.31 The QuickEntry window opens ready for you to make an entry.

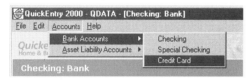

Figure 4.32 Use the Accounts menu to switch to another account.

Using Data Entry Helpers

Another useful data entry tool you should know about is QuickEntry. QuickEntry (found only in Quicken Deluxe) allows you to enter transactions without even opening Quicken.

If you enter transactions every day (and even if you don't), QuickEntry can reduce the time it takes. This small application opens quickly and lets you enter data into all of your bank, credit card, and cash account registers. You enter transactions into QuickEntry exactly the same way you would into Quicken. QuickEntry stores the data in your Quicken data file and adds it to your Quicken registers the next time you open the Quicken program.

To use QuickEntry:

1. Click on the QuickEntry 2000 shortcut icon on the desktop (**Figure 4.30**). (Quicken added the shortcut here when you installed the program.)

   The QuickEntry 2000 window appears (**Figure 4.31**) showing the last register you had open.

2. From the Accounts menu (**Figure 4.32**), you can choose another account to which you want to enter data.

   After you make the change, the Ending Balance for that account appears in QuickEntry's lower right corner.

3. Enter transactions as you would in any Quicken register, clicking the Enter button after each entry.

4. When you're done making entries, choose File > Exit, or click the Start Quicken button in the global bar to switch to the full version of Quicken.

AUTOMATING YOUR TRANSACTIONS

5

If your financial situation is anything like mine, you find yourself repeating similar transactions over and over. For example, you probably make a rent or mortgage payment every month and deposit your paycheck once a month or every other week. You probably also pay many of the same bills every month—to the phone company, to your electric utility, to your supermarket for groceries, whatever. You could simply type in all of that stuff again and again and again, but why bother? That's the kind of repetitive dog work for which computers were designed. Using the QuickFill feature in Quicken, you can let your computer remember and enter the boring stuff for you.

QuickFill watches over your shoulder as you type information into an account register or onto a check. When the information you're typing matches a previous transaction, QuickFill enters the rest of the transaction for you. QuickFill can remember all or part of a transaction, so you can use it to remember and enter transactions whose amounts stay the same every month (such as your rent or mortgage payment) or transactions that can change each month (like the electric bill).

In this chapter, you'll learn how to use QuickFill to make entering transactions easier, and you'll learn how to memorize, edit, enter, and delete QuickFill transactions.

How QuickFill Works

Let's face it—there's nothing especially fun or glamorous about entering your transactions into an account register. In fact, it can be downright dull. QuickFill is an important tool that helps you get information into Quicken fast and with a minimum of boredom.

Every time you enter a transaction in your account register or on a check, Quicken adds the information to the Memorized Transaction list. Then, when you create a new entry, Quicken compares the information in the Memorized Transaction list to what you're typing. As soon as it finds a match, QuickFill fills in the rest of the transaction for you. If QuickFill's guess is correct, probably all you'll need to do is change the amount of that particular check. If QuickFill guesses wrong, you keep typing and your entry will replace QuickFill's guess.

You can also manually add transactions to the Memorized Transaction list by selecting a transaction and telling Quicken to memorize it. You can view, use, edit, or delete QuickFill transactions via the Memorized Transaction List window (**Figure 5.1**).

✔ Tips

- QuickFill is turned on by default, but you can turn it off. Choose Edit > Options > Register to open the Register Options window and click the QuickFill tab (**Figure 5.2**). Clear the check box next to "Complete Fields Using Previous Entries."

- You can turn off automatic updating of the QuickFill list by clearing the box next to the "Auto Memorize New Transactions" option. And you can stop the memorized transactions from appearing uninvited by clearing the box marked "Drop Down Lists on Field Entry."

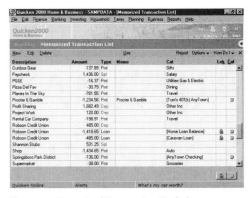

Figure 5.1 Memorized Transaction List helps you save a tremendous amount of time and keystrokes.

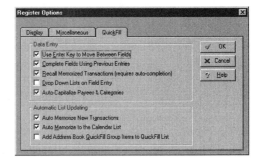

Figure 5.2 You can turn QuickFill features on or off in the Register Options window.

QuickFill Tab Options

In the Register Options window, you'll see two sections: Data Entry and Automatic List Updating. Each section offers several options for data entry and list updating.

The Data Entry section includes the following options:

♦ **Use Enter Key to Move Between Fields**. Normally, you'll press the [Tab] key to move between the fields in a register. But if you prefer to use the [Enter] key, check this box.

♦ **Complete Fields Using Previous Entries**. This option watches as you type and fills in a field as soon as it finds a match in your previous entries.

♦ **Recall Memorized Transactions**. This feature fills in all of the fields in an entry when QuickFill sees a match. It makes recurring bills easy to enter; usually, all you have to change is the amount of the check, if that.

♦ **Drop Down Lists on Field Entry**. This option displays a drop-down list as soon as you enter a field, so you can either keep typing until you get a match or select from the drop-down list directly.

♦ **Auto-Capitalize Payees & Categories**. This handy feature makes it a bit faster to enter data by automatically adding capital letters to your entries.

The Automatic List Updating section includes the following options:

♦ **Auto Memorize New Transactions**. If this is checked, new transactions you enter will be added automatically to the Memorized Transaction List.

♦ **Auto Memorize to the Calendar List**. This option adds transactions automatically to the Financial Calendar (see Chapter 7).

♦ **Add Financial Address Book Items to QuickFill List**. Click this option to add items you enter in the Financial Address Book to the Memorized Transaction List. This option is available only in Quicken Deluxe.

How QuickFill Works

Memorizing Transactions

Most of the time, you won't need to do anything to memorize a transaction and add it to the QuickFill Memorized Transaction List. Quicken does it for you automatically. You can see for yourself—assuming that you have already entered some data into Quicken. Open the Memorized Transaction List by choosing Lists > Memorized Transaction (or pressing Ctrl T), and check out the automatically memorized transactions.

Sometimes, however, you'll want to ask Quicken to memorize a transaction manually, usually because you want to lock or unlock the transaction. The little padlocks that appear in the Lck column in **Figure 5.3** indicate locked transactions. You can unlock memorized transactions so that QuickFill will memorize any changes that you make, or you can lock transactions so that the Memorized Transaction List entry will not update if you make any changes to the register entry.

You would typically use unlocked transactions for items written to the same payee but containing different details. For example, you might often write checks at the same supermarket, but the amount and even the category will probably be different for every check.

You'll want to use a locked QuickFill transaction for checks you write to the same payee for which the details hardly if ever change, such as a car or mortgage payment. You can still change the amount of the transaction in the register or on the check; but the change in the register won't affect the memorized amount stored in a locked QuickFill transaction.

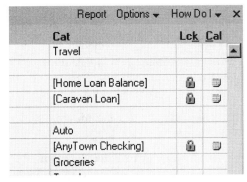

Figure 5.3 Quicken indicates locked transactions with a padlock symbol in the Memorized Transaction List.

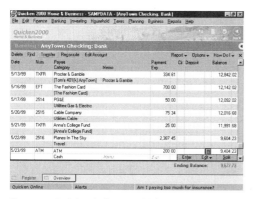

Figure 5.4 Quicken indicates which transaction is selected in a register by adding a border around the transaction.

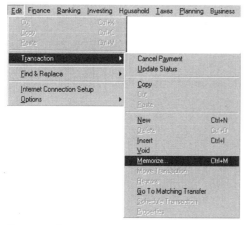

Figure 5.5 Choose Edit > Transaction > Memorize or press Ctrl M to memorize a transaction manually.

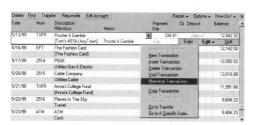

Figure 5.6 The Edit pop-up menu in the register also gives you the option of memorizing the current transaction.

To memorize a QuickFill transaction manually:

1. In your account register, select a transaction by clicking it.

   Quicken adds a border around the transaction you selected (**Figure 5.4**).

2. Choose Edit > Transaction > Memorize (**Figure 5.5**), or press Ctrl M.

✔ Tip

- You can also memorize a transaction in the middle of making your register entry by clicking the Edit button in the register line and choosing Memorize Transaction (**Figure 5.6**).

MEMORIZING TRANSACTIONS

Using Memorized Transactions

QuickFill usually works unobtrusively, automatically popping in information as you enter transactions in account registers or on checks. But you can also use the Memorized Transaction List in a manual fashion to help you add transactions. You do this by keeping the Memorized Transaction list open while entering data.

Why would you want to do this? Here's one example. I use three telephone lines in my house. One line is personal and the other two are business related, so I track expenditures on all three separately. Naturally, the same phone company maintains all three lines, so the payee is the same. Using QuickFill in the usual fashion, I wouldn't be able to track which QuickFill transactions cover the personal line and which transactions cover the business lines. Instead, I can open the Memorized Transaction List: Each transaction includes a Memo field, in which I've indicated the type of phone line to which the QuickFill transaction applies.

To use the Memorized Transaction List to help enter transactions:

1. With your account register open, choose Banking > Memorized Transaction List.

   The Memorized Transaction List window appears (**Figure 5.7**).

2. Scroll through the Memorized Transaction List until you find the transaction that you want to use, and then click on the transaction to highlight it.

   Click the Use button to transfer the contents of the transaction to the open account register.

   or

   Double-click the transaction to enter it in the account register.

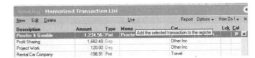

Figure 5.7 The Memorized Transaction List window.

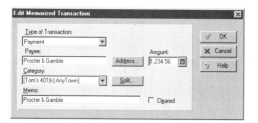

Figure 5.8 You can edit a transaction in the Edit Memorized Transaction dialog box.

Editing QuickFill Transactions

You can change any part of a QuickFill transaction, although you won't usually need to do so. Most often, you'll clear the amount of a transaction, and then lock the transaction so that in future items involving the same payee, you'll simply fill in the amount of the check.

To edit a QuickFill transaction:

1. Choose Banking > Memorized Transaction List.

   The Memorized Transaction List window appears.

2. Single-click on the transaction to select it.

3. Click the Edit button at the top of the Memorized Transaction List window.

   The Edit Memorized Transaction dialog box appears (**Figure 5.8**).

4. Make changes as needed in the Type of Transaction, Payee, Amount, Category, and Memo fields. Notice that, if needed, you can use split transactions by clicking the Split button (see Chapter 4).

5. To replace the transaction with your changes, click the OK button. To back out of the window without saving changes, click the Cancel button.

To lock or unlock a QuickFill transaction:

1. Follow steps 1 and 2 in the preceding list.

2. To lock a transaction, click in the Lck column of the transaction. A padlock icon will appear.

    or

    To unlock the transaction, click the padlock to toggle it off.

✔ Tips

- If you leave Memorized Transaction unlocked, Quicken replaces the amount of the check in the transaction every time you use the QuickFill entry. The next time you use that QuickFill entry, the amount of the last check you wrote to that payee will appear. This makes it easy to determine whether your spending with that payee has changed drastically. If it has, you have a chance to either rethink your spending pattern or check for an error in the current month's bill. I once found a $75 error in a utility bill in this fashion.

- If a loan transaction is listed in your Memorized Transaction List, you won't be able to edit it from the Memorized Transaction List window. You'll need to go to the Loans window (choose Household > Loans). For more about changing loan information, see Chapter 12.

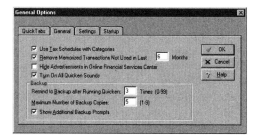

Figure 5.9 Use the General Options window to clear out old, unused memorized transactions.

Deleting Memorized Transactions

You might choose to get rid of a memorized transaction because it lists a payee that you dealt with only once or because you want to eliminate duplicate entries.

To delete a memorized transaction:

1. In the Memorized Transaction List window, single-click on the transaction that you want to eliminate.

   Quicken highlights the transaction.

2. Click the Delete button at the top of the window.

✔ Tip

- There's a limit of 2,000 transactions in the Memorized Transaction List. If you use all 2,000 slots, you might need to delete some memorized transactions. To clear out older transactions automatically, choose Options > Quicken Program to open the General Options window. Then click the General tab (**Figure 5.9**). Click the "Remove Memorized Transactions Not Used in Last [blank] Months" check box. You can fill in the amount in the Months field with an appropriate number.

Writing and Printing Checks

Just to avoid any possible confusion, this chapter is about writing checks that you intend to print from Quicken on preprinted check forms. Checks that you write by hand should be entered in your checking account register, as discussed in Chapter 4.

If you don't already use Quicken to print your checks on preprinted check forms, you should reconsider. While researching this book, I found that a surprising number of people don't use the program's printing abilities. If you're one of those folks, you're missing out on a lot of convenience. Consider this: When you write a check in your regular checkbook, you first fill out the check. Then you have to type all the same information into Quicken's check register. That's double work. If you let Quicken print the check, you enter the information once and you're done.

Using Quicken to print your checks can also avoid errors. Before I started printing checks, I'd discover (usually after chasing numbers for a half hour when balancing my checkbook) that I had typed an incorrect amount for a hand-written check into Quicken's register. But when you write a check in Quicken, there's no chance of a pesky typo wasting your time later because Quicken automatically enters each amount into its register. It makes checkbook balancing much faster.

To write a check:

1. Open the Write Checks window by choosing Banking > Write Checks, or by pressing [Ctrl][W].

   The Write Checks window for your main checking account appears (**Figure 6.1**).

   Note: Make sure that you're writing a check in the correct account by checking the tabs at the bottom of the Write Checks window. If necessary, scroll the tabs until you find the account you want, and then select it.

2. In the Write Checks window, today's date is entered for you and highlighted. If you want to change the date, type in a new date.

   or

   Click the Calendar button in the Write Checks window and a small calendar will pop up (**Figure 6.2**). Click on the new date in the small calendar window to add that date to the check.

3. Type in the name of the payee.

   As you type, QuickFill will anticipate and fill in the payee's name if what you're typing is similar to a name that appears on a previously written check. (See Chapter 5 for more about QuickFill.) QuickFill also fills in the same amount that appeared on the last check you wrote to the payee, which is handy for checks that you write each month for the same amount.

4. Press the [Tab] key to move on if the amount is correct. If it's not correct, fill in the amount of the check.

   On the next line, Quicken turns the amount you entered into its text form. (For $42.76, for example, Quicken enters Forty-two and 76/100, and then it adds asterisks to fill out the extra space.)

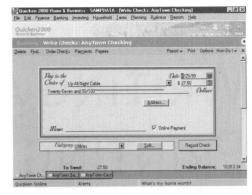

Figure 6.1 The Write Checks window looks like a real check, and you fill it out in much the same way that you fill out a regular check.

Figure 6.2 You can choose a date for the check from the calendar pop-up window.

Writing Checks by Hand

When you're away from home, you can write checks with the checkbook that your bank provided when you opened your account or you can use your preprinted computer checks and fill them out by hand. I like to use my regular bank checkbook and enter the information into Quicken when I return home. I differentiate between the checks that Quicken prints and ones I hand write by using two widely different sets of check numbers for each kind of check. For example, I started my computer checks at 1000 and my handwritten checks start in the 4000 range. Quicken has no problem dealing with different sets of check numbers.

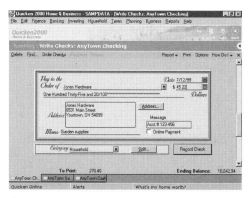

Figure 6.3 Your completed check should look something like this.

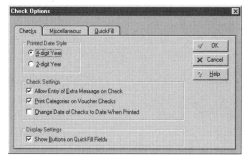

Figure 6.4 Use the Check Options dialog box to allow extra messages in a check's message field.

Message box

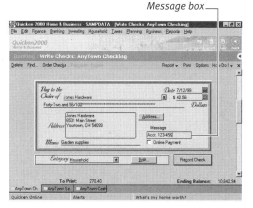

Figure 6.5 Type your account number on a check and it will appear in the extra message line.

5. Enter the name and address of the payee in the Address field (optional). You'll want to enter an address if you plan to use window envelopes. To copy and paste the payee's name into the first line of the Address field, press the single quotation mark (`'`) key.

6. Fill in the Memo field to record a memo about this check (optional).

7. If QuickFill entered the appropriate payee in step 2, it probably filled in the Category field as well. If the category is correct, move on to the next step; otherwise type in the appropriate category or use the Category pop-up menu to select one.

8. Click the Record Check button or press the ⟨Enter⟩ key. The completed check should look similar to that shown in **Figure 6.3.** Quicken adds the check to a list of Checks to be printed.

✔ Tips

■ If you mail your printed check in a windowed mailing envelope, the Memo line may be visible through the window, so adding confidential account numbers to the Memo line would be unsuitable. Instead, choose Edit > Options > Write Checks, and in the Check Options dialog box, click "Allow Entry of Extra Message on Check" (**Figure 6.4**) and then click OK. A message box will appear on the check. You can fill in this note line from the Write Checks window only (**Figure 6.5**); the account register doesn't show it. This note line also won't appear in the envelope window.

■ To memorize transactions in the Write Checks window as well as in the account register, choose Edit > Transaction > Memorize or press ⟨Ctrl⟩⟨M⟩.

To edit a check:

1. Scroll through your unsent checks using the scroll bar along the right side of the Write Checks window until you find the check you want to change.

   All checks are available in this window until printed or sent as an online payment.

2. Edit the information.

3. Click the Record Check button or press the (Enter) key to save your work.

✔ Tip

- If you prefer, you can edit the check by making changes in the account register. (See Chapter 4 for how to use the account register.) After you print a check, it disappears from the Write Checks window and is entered in the account register. Note that the check is accessible only from the account register after it has been printed.

To delete a check:

1. Locate up the check you want to delete using the scroll bar.

2. Choose Edit > Transaction > Delete, or press `Ctrl` `D`.

   or

   Click the Delete button at the top of the Write check window.

   Quicken will pop up a dialog box asking if you're sure you want to delete this check.

3. Click the OK button to confirm the deletion.

✔ Tips

- You can neither delete a check nor edit check information from the Write Checks window after the check has been printed. If you need to change or delete check information after you have printed a check, you must access the information from the account register. See the section on printing, later in this chapter, for more information.

- Looking to void a check? You have to do that in the account register. See "Voiding Transactions" in Chapter 4 for more information.

Address Maintenance

Quicken 2000 keeps track of the addresses of your Payees in three places: in the Scheduled Transactions List, in the Memorized Transactions list, and in the Financial Address Book. When you make a change to a payee's address in one list, the changes are automatically reflected in the other two lists.

To keep the addresses synchronized, you must be consistent when you're creating addresses. In particular, you should keep the number of lines in an address to five or less, and the last line of the address should only be a zip or postal code or the words USA, US, United States of America, United States, America, or Canada. Other entries will result in a failure to synchronize addresses.

Getting Ready to Print

After you have entered your checks for printing in the Write Checks window or in the account register, you're almost ready to print. First you must set up Quicken to print your checks.

To set up Quicken to print:

1. In Quicken, choose File > Printer Setup > For Printing Checks.

   The Check Printer Setup dialog box appears (**Figure 6.6**).

2. If more than one printer is available to you, choose the one you want to use from the Printer drop-down list.

3. Unless you have a continuous-feed printer, leave the Page-oriented radio button selected.

4. Select the check style (standard, voucher, or wallet) from the Check Style drop-down list.

5. Depending on how your particular printer feeds paper, choose one of the three printing style alignments when printing one or two checks.

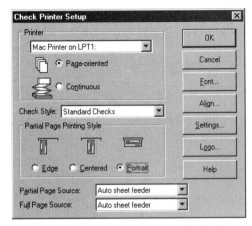

Figure 6.6 You usually need to use the Check Printer Setup window only once.

GETTING READY TO PRINT

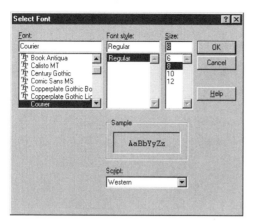

Figure 6.7 You can use any font installed on your system on a check, but you're probably better off using a dull, boring font like Arial or Times New Roman so that your checks can be easily read. Leave the creativity to another arena.

6. Choose different paper sources for full or partial pages of checks (optional).

7. Click the Font button, which brings up the Select Font dialog box (**Figure 6.7**). Choose the font, font style, and font size you want printed on your checks, and then click OK.

8. In the Check Printer Setup dialog box, click the OK button to save your settings.

✔ Tips

- For most printers, Quicken's default settings will do just fine.

- Clicking the Logo button in the Check Printer Setup dialog box allows you to print an image, such as a logo, on your checks. The image must be in .BMP format.

- Clicking the Align button in the Check Printer Setup dialog box lets you tweak where on the page Quicken will print.

GETTING READY TO PRINT

Printing Checks

Now that you've set up Quicken's printing functions, it's finally time to print. Note that most of the setup needs to be done only once; you'll just be printing merrily away.

To print checks:

1. Make sure the checks are positioned correctly in your printer tray. You might want to run a test on some plain paper before you print on real checks for the first time.

2. Verify that your printer is turned on and that it is online.

3. Open the account from which you want to print checks.

4. Choose File > Print Checks, or press Ctrl P.

   The Select Checks to Print dialog box appears (**Figure 6.8**), telling you how many checks are ready to print.

5. The first check number should match the first number of the checks that you put in the printer. If it doesn't match, change it.

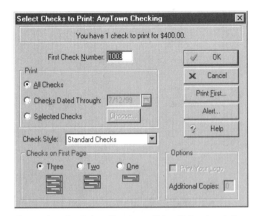

Figure 6.8 The Select Checks to Print dialog box tells you how many checks are set to print.

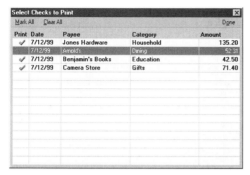

Figure 6.9 To print particular checks, select them in the Select Checks to Print window.

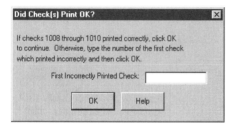

Figure 6.10 Quicken needs reassurance that your checks printed correctly. Soothe it by clicking the OK button.

6. In the Print section of the dialog box, add a date in the Checks Dated Through box to print all checks written up to this date. You'll probably use this option most often.

   or

   Click the Selected Checks radio button and then the Choose button to open the Select Checks to Print window (**Figure 6.9**). In the Print column, click to add a checkmark next to the checks that you want to print, and then click Done.

7. Click the Print button in the Printer dialog box to start printing checks.

8. After the checks have been printed, Quicken will ask you whether all the checks printed correctly (**Figure 6.10**). If they did, click OK and Quicken will enter the check numbers into the account register.

9. If any of the checks did not print correctly (usually because of a printer problem), type in the number of the first incorrectly printed check. Fix the printer problem, and then start again at step 4 above to print the remaining checks.

✔ Tip

- You can reprint a check at any time (if a payee loses a check, for example). Just replace the check number in your register with the word *PRINT*, and click the Record button. Then print the check normally.

PRINTING CHECKS

71

Ordering Checks

You can buy checks preprinted with your name, address, bank name and account number, check numbers, and any other information required by your bank. These checks are designed for use in laser printers and ink-jet printers (you can also order continuous checks for dot-matrix printers), and they generally come in one of three styles:

◆ Standard Checks are sized for use in a business-size envelope and come three to a page (**Figure 6.11**).

◆ Voucher Checks are good for payroll and accounts payable use; you get one check per page, with two check stubs that you can keep or send out with the check as needed (**Figure 6.12**).

◆ Wallet Checks are smaller than standard checks (so that they can, not surprisingly, fit into your wallet) and include a stub for recording check information when writing a check by hand (**Figure 6.13**).

After you decide which style to use, have your current checkbook ready (you'll need it for the bank information and your account number) and order your checks. You can order checks from Intuit, although they tend to charge more than some other companies. Many other business supply companies can provide checks and save you some money. See **Table 6.1** for some suggestions.

Figure 6.11 Standard checks are the most convenient and are used by most people.

Figure 6.12 Voucher checks are good if you need a paper trail of check stubs. But for most of us, the less paper, the better.

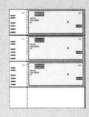

Figure 6.13 Wallet style checks make sense if you want to carry your computer checks with you.

Table 6.1

Sources for Computer Checks

COMPANY	PHONE NUMBER	URL
Intuit	800-787-6748	www.intuitmarketplace.com
NEBS	800-225-6380	www.nebs.com
Checks for Less	800-325-5568	www.checksforless.com
PC Checks	800-322-5317	www.pcchecks.com
Sensible Solutions	888-852-4325	www.sensible-solutions.com

PRINTING CHECKS

USING THE FINANCIAL CALENDAR

When a bill gets paid is often as important as the amount of the payment. Because many of your financial transactions are time sensitive, Quicken gives you a tool that lets you see your transactions over time: the Financial Calendar. With this calendar, you can schedule future transactions and set up recurring transactions that you need to pay on a regular schedule, such as mortgage payments or utility bills. Quicken can enter scheduled transactions automatically, saving you the drudgery of data entry. The Calendar can also remind you of upcoming payments and give you a quick visual overview of how you spend your money each month.

Two other Quicken features work with the Financial Calendar: the Scheduled Transactions list and Billminder. Scheduled transactions are memorized transactions (see Chapter 5) that get entered automatically when they're due. Billminder pops up when you start Windows and reminds you of scheduled transactions.

With the help of the Financial Calendar, scheduled transactions, and Billminder, you won't have any excuse for forgetting to pay your bills on time. In the Deluxe versions of Quicken, you'll also see your scheduled transactions on the Quicken My Finances Home Page (see Chapter 8).

Working with the Financial Calendar

To display the Financial Calendar, choose Finance > Financial Calendar or press (Ctrl)(K). The Financial Calendar will appear (**Figure 7.1**), with the current day highlighted and the financial transactions you've made in the current month listed in black text on their respective dates. Transactions that have been scheduled but have not yet been paid are displayed in blue.

The controls at the top of the Financial Calendar (Previous Month, Go to Date, and Next Month) let you change the month displayed. The right side of the calendar shows the Memorized Transactions list, which lets you drag and drop transactions onto the calendar, turning them into scheduled transactions.

To add a new transaction in the Calendar:

1. In the Calendar, double-click the date on which you wish to schedule a transaction.

   The Transactions Due window for that date appears (**Figure 7.2**).

2. Click the New button in the Transactions Due window.

   The New Transaction dialog box appears (**Figure 7.3**).

3. Click the down arrow in the Account to Use area to see the Account drop-down list. Choose the account to which you'll apply the transaction.

4. From the Type of Transaction drop-down list, choose Payment, Deposit, Print Check, or Online Payment.

Note   Previous   Go To   Next   Memorized Transactions List
Month   Date   Month

Figure 7.1 If you prefer, you can do all your data entry in the Financial Calendar.

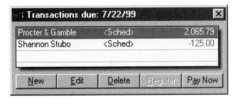

Figure 7.2 The Transactions Due window shows you the transactions scheduled for a particular date.

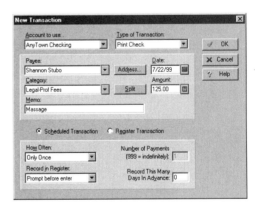

Figure 7.3 The New Transaction dialog box lets you enter any sort of transaction except investment transactions or loan payments.

Figure 7.4 Use the How Often drop-down list to select the frequency of a transaction.

5. Enter the Payee's name.

   As you're typing in the name, QuickFill looks at other names that you've entered previously in this area. If it finds a match, it adds the name. If this name is incorrect, you can simply keep typing to change it.

6. By default, the current date appears in the Date field. You can leave this date as is or change it to another date.

7. Type in the category or open the Category drop-down list to select the category of the transaction. If necessary, click the Split button to enter a split category. (See Chapter 4 for more about splitting transactions.)

8. In the Amount field, enter the amount of the payment.

9. Enter a Memo about the transaction (optional).

10. If you want to enter the transaction into the register immediately, click the Register Transaction radio button and skip to step 14. If you're scheduling a future transaction, click the Scheduled Transaction button.

11. If this is a one-time transaction, leave the How Often drop-down list set to Only Once.

    or

    If this will be a recurring transaction, select how often it will recur from the How Often drop-down list (**Figure 7.4**).

    (continued)

12. In the Number of Payments box, enter either the number of payments or *999* for an indefinite number of payments.

13. In the Record in Register drop-down list, choose either Prompt Before Enter or Automatically Enter. If you want Quicken to remind you or automatically enter the information in advance of the date you selected, fill in the Record This Many Days In Advance field with a number of days.

14. Click the OK button to save the transaction.

To edit a transaction:

1. In the Financial Calendar, double-click the day containing the transaction that you want to edit. The Transactions Due window for that day appears, as shown in **Figure 7.5.**

2. Click the transaction that you want to change, and then click the Edit button. The Edit Scheduled Transaction dialog box, which looks and acts exactly like the New Transaction dialog box, appears.

3. Make any changes you want, and then click the OK button.

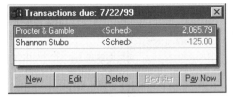

Figure 7.5 You can add, change, or delete scheduled transactions for that day in the Transactions Due window.

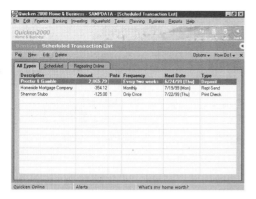

Figure 7.6 You can check all of your upcoming transactions in the Scheduled Transaction List.

To view scheduled transactions:

1. Choose Banking > Scheduled Transaction List, or press (Ctrl)(J).

   The Scheduled Transaction List window appears, showing your upcoming transactions (**Figure 7.6**).

   The window shows recurring transactions along with their frequency, so rather than listing every future instance of a transaction that happens twice a month, it lists just the transaction's next due date and "Twice a month" in the Frequency column.

2. Create a new scheduled transaction or edit and delete existing transactions using the buttons at the top of the Scheduled Transaction List window.

To delete a scheduled transaction:

1. In the Financial Calendar, double-click the day that contains a transaction that you want to delete.

   The Transactions Due window for that day appears (refer to **Figure 7.5**).

2. Click the transaction to select it.

3. Click the Delete button.

4. Quicken will ask you to confirm the deletion. Click the OK button to delete the transaction.

✔ Tip

- Remember that entering a transaction in the Calendar also enters it in an account register.

Changing a Transaction Pattern

Sometimes you'll want to pay a scheduled transaction in advance of when you would normally make a payment, or you'll want to skip a payment. For example, if you happened to get a big tax refund (wouldn't that be nice?), you might want to spend some or all of that windfall on paying off some bills early.

To pay or skip a scheduled transaction:

1. Open the Scheduled Transaction List by choosing Banking > Scheduled Transaction List or pressing [Ctrl][J] (refer to **Figure 7.6**).

2. Double-click the transaction that you wish to pay or skip.

   The Record Scheduled Transaction dialog box opens (**Figure 7.7**).

3. To make an unscheduled payment, fill in the Date, Amount, and Number information and then click the Record button.

4. If you want to skip the payment, click the Skip button.

   Quicken closes the window and moves the next payment forward to the next scheduled payment time.

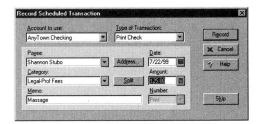

Figure 7.7 You can make payments in advance—or skip a payment—in the Record Scheduled Transaction window.

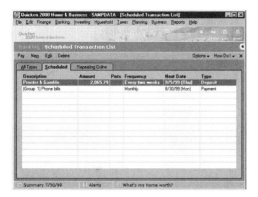

Figure 7.8 The Create Scheduled Transaction window opens, with the Group button on the right.

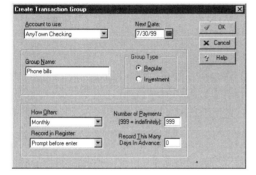

Figure 7.9 Create new groups in the Create Transaction Group dialog box.

Using Transaction Groups

It's often more convenient to pay your bills in batches. For example, because I have three telephone lines at my house, I receive three different bills. I prefer to pay all three bills at the same time, so I've created a transaction group in the Calendar that automatically enters three separate transactions simultaneously.

To create a transaction group:

1. Choose Banking > Scheduled Transaction List. The Scheduled Transaction List window appears.

2. Click the Scheduled tab at the top of the list to open it (**Figure 7.8**).

3. Click the New button at the top of the window.

   The Create Scheduled Transaction window opens.

4. Click the Group button. The Create Transaction Group dialog box appears (**Figure 7.9**).

5. From the Account to Use drop-down list, choose the account from which you will be making the payments.

6. Enter the Next Date for the transaction group.

7. In the Group Name field, type a name for the transaction group.

8. Set the frequency for the recurring group transaction in the How Often field. If there are a set number of payments, enter this amount in the Number of Payments box. Also set whether you want to enter the group automatically in your register or whether you want to approve the entry.

(continued)

9. Click the OK button. The Assign Transactions to Group window appears (**Figure 7.10**).

10. Double-click each transaction that you want to include in the group. This adds the number of the group into the Grp column next to each selected transaction. If you make a mistake and need to deselect a transaction, double-click it again.

11. Click the close box (the x) in the upper right corner of the window. The Scheduled Transaction List will now show an entry for the group you just created.

To use a transaction group:

1. In the Scheduled Transaction List window, select a transaction group.

2. Click the Pay button. The Record Transaction Group dialog box appears (**Figure 7.11**).

3. Make sure that the settings in the dialog box are correct, and then click the Record button.

Quicken will make the appropriate entries in the account registers and open those registers for your inspection.

4. If necessary, edit the transactions in the registers in the usual fashion.

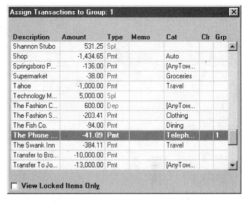

Figure 7.10 In this window, you assign memorized transactions to groups.

Figure 7.11 The Record Transaction Group dialog box lets you add multiple entries to the account register in one step.

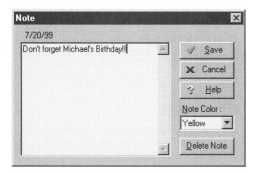

Figure 7.12 You can include any text that you want in the Calendar's Note window.

Note Icon

Figure 7.13 Click the note icon to recall your note.

Adding Calendar Notes

In addition to showing transactions, the Calendar can also contain notes, similar to yellow sticky notes, that contain virtually any information—from personal notes, to to-do lists, to additional notes on the financial transactions for that day.

To create a calendar note:

1. In the Calendar window, select a date for which you wish to add a note.

2. At the top left of the Calendar window, click the Note button.
   The Note window for that date appears.

3. Enter the text for the note (**Figure 7.12**), and change the note color if you like.

4. Click the Save button.

5. Quicken adds a small note icon to the day for which you created the note (**Figure 7.13**). To read the note in the future, click the note icon.

To delete a calendar note:

1. Open the note by clicking on it.

2. Click the Delete Note button.

Using Billminder

You can set Billminder to alert you of scheduled transactions as soon as you start up Windows. (Don't worry, you can also turn it off if you want.) Quicken doesn't have to be running for Billminder to do its job. Once Billminder pops up, you can either run Quicken and deal with the reminders or you can skip the reminders until the next time you start up your computer.

To turn Billminder on:

1. Choose Finance > Reminders.

   The Quicken Reminders window appears.

2. From the Options menu at the top of the window, choose Billminder, and then make sure that you've checked the box next to Show Billminder when starting Windows (**Figure 7.14**).

   The next time you start up your computer, the Billminder window will appear (**Figure 7.15**).

To set the reminder date:

1. Choose Edit > Options > Reminders.

   The Days Shown window appears (**Figure 7.16**).

2. Enter the number of days in advance of the event that you want Quicken to remind you about the event, and then click the OK button.

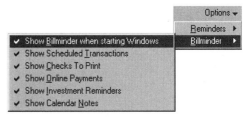

Figure 7.14 Billminder won't let you forget upcoming transactions. All you have to do is remember to turn Billminder on in the first place.

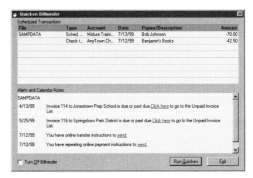

Figure 7.15 Billminder runs when you start Windows and shows you what's coming up in your financial life.

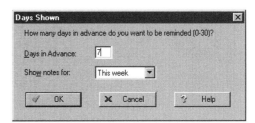

Figure 7.16 Enter the number of days in advance that you want reminders in the Days Shown window.

THE MY FINANCES HOME PAGE

8

Quicken offers you a lot of control over your finances and a virtual avalanche of supporting data that you can use to assess where you are in terms of reaching your financial goals. But this wealth of information, while useful, can also be overwhelming. It can take a long time to plow through several reports and registers to get the big picture of your investments, assets, and liabilities.

Quicken's My Finances Home Page organizes all of your financial information onto one page. From this page, you can get the big financial picture and evaluate how you are doing in any personal finance area without having to rummage through different reports. The My Finances Home Page includes tables, graphs, and hypertext links that let you perform a whole range of Quicken tasks.

In this chapter, you'll learn how to use and customize Quicken's My Finances Home Page to get the information that you need.

What's on the My Finances Home Page?

The main My Finances Home Page window is originally set to display six Activity Centers of general interest (**Figure 8.1**):

◆ **Learn About Quicken** puts the key feature of the Help menu on the desktop.

◆ **Alerts & Reminders** remind you of financial events that you might otherwise miss. For example, you can set up an alert to remind you when it's time to reorder checks.

◆ The **Accounts** list gives you a rundown of the current balances in all of your accounts.

◆ **Scheduled Transactions** lets you know what automatic payments are coming up.

◆ The **Watch List** gives you the current prices of selected securities and lets you know what securities have had the best and worst performance over the last 30 days.

◆ **Download Summary** shows what information has been downloaded from the Internet, including stock information and balances from your online accounts.

Quicken is set to display the My Finances Home Page when you first start up the Quicken program, and you can open it at any time.

You can customize what appears on your My Finances Home Page by adding, deleting, or rearranging new components up to the limit of 16 different tools on a single page.

Figure 8.1 The My Finances Home Page shows you up to 16 areas of useful financial information.

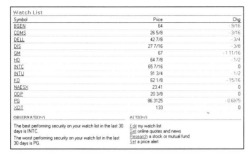

Figure 8.2 The Watch List shows the securities and their prices in the display area, tells you the best and worst performers in the Observations area, and lets you research a stock or update prices in the Actions area.

Figure 8.3 The Customize menu allows you to change what features are displayed on this page or to create a new one.

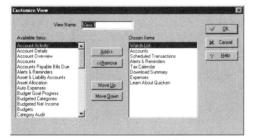

Figure 8.4 Set which financial tools you want to display on the Home Page with the Add and Remove buttons.

Each component's display area shows some aspect of your financial world, and an Actions area lets you get more information or do something related to that component. Some components also have Observations areas, which analyze the data. In **Figure 8.2**, the Watch List shows the securities and their prices in the display area, tells you the best and worst performers in the Observations area, and lets you research a stock or update prices in the Actions area.

Clicking on an underlined link in the Actions area triggers that function. If the display area contains a graph, holding the mouse cursor over a graph segment shows you the dollar amount of that segment, and double-clicking it opens a more detailed graph of the underlying data.

To open the Quicken Home Page:

◆ Choose Finances > My Finances

or

Click My Finances on the QuickTab bar.

To customize your Home Page:

1. From the My Finances Home Page, choose Customize, which is a pop-up menu (even though it doesn't look like it) (**Figure 8.3**).

2. From the pop-up menu, choose Customize this View.
   The Customize View window appears (**Figure 8.4**).

3. Use the Add or Remove buttons to move items back and forth between the Available Items and Chosen Items columns.

4. To rearrange the financial tools on the page, use the Move Up and Move Down buttons.

5. Click OK to save your changes.

To keep the My Finances Home Page from appearing at startup:

1. Choose Edit > Options > Quicken Program. The General Options window appears.

2. Click the Startup tab (**Figure 8.5**).

3. Click the Reminders When Starting Quicken to have the program open with that feature or the None radio button to have it open with the screen it was showing when you shut it down last time.

4. Click OK to save your changes.

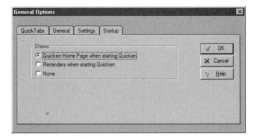

Figure 8.5 You can keep Home Page from displaying at startup—although it's really too useful to miss.

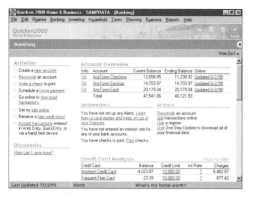

Figure 8.6 Of all the Activity Centers, you'll probably use the Banking Center the most, as it gives you a comprehensive overview of your checking, savings, and credit card accounts.

Figure 8.7 You can get an analysis of your investment performance in the Investing Center.

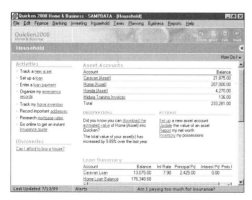

Figure 8.8 Links in the Household Center let you retrieve information from the Internet about refinancing your mortgage and other debt-restructuring strategies.

Using the Activity Centers

Each of the six Activity Centers is a separate Home Page for a sector of your economic life. You display a particular Center by choosing it from the menu (for example choose Banking > Banking Center to open its Home Page) or from the QuickTabs buttons.

The Activity Centers and the Financial Home Page have a similar layout: a number of information display areas, with action and observation links that help you use the information they present, and a How Do I? button on the tool bar that you can click for general guidance on using the Quicken program. Here's a rundown on each of the Activitiy Centers:

◆ **The Banking Center** (**Figure 8.6**) gives you an overview of your cash, checking, savings, money market, and credit card accounts. It will show you information such as which accounts you haven't reconciled recently, and it can show you an analysis of your credit card spending.

◆ In the **Investing Center** (**Figure 8.7**), you can take a look at your overall investment situation. Get a high-level view of your investments, open up the Portfolio View, or zoom into the Detail View of a particular security.

◆ The **Household Center** (**Figure 8.8**) zooms in on your two most important assets. It also lets you deal with any other liabilities.

(continued)

◆ The **Taxes Center** (**Figure 8.9**) lets you know how much tax you have paid in the year to date, estimates how much you might owe in taxes next year, and lets you know important tax deadlines.

◆ The **Planning Center** (**Figure 8.10**) focuses on savings, your net worth, and activities such as budgeting, debt reduction, and setting your savings goals. This is the Activity Center you'll turn to for links about setting up retirement accounts and other long-term savings plans.

◆ The **Reports and Graphs Center** (**Figure 8.11**) makes it easier for you to compile all the data in your Quicken files into comprehensible forms.

◆ If you're using Quicken Home & Business, one more Activity Center is available to you. The **Small Business Center** (**Figure 8.12**) shows your unpaid invoices, a summary of payables and receivables, and a year-to-date profit and loss graph that shows you at a glance how you're doing.

✔ Tips

■ You can't customize the Activity Centers, unlike the My Finances Home Page.

■ Whenever you see an underlined account name in one of the Activity Centers' Home Pages (or on the My Finances Home Page, for that matter), it represents a link, just as it appears on a Web page. In this case, clicking it opens a corresponding register for that account.

■ Pay attention to the Observations areas; they often have useful reminders and smart analyses.

Figure 8.9 Find out your estimated tax liability in the Taxes Center.

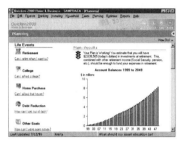

Figure 8.10 The Planning Center's Links section gives you access to a ton of retirement information on Intuit's Web site.

Figure 8.11 The Reports and Graphs Center can produce both simple and complex presentations.

Figure 8.12 The Small Business Center makes life easier for the entrepreneur—you can see the most important data about your business at a glance.

Using One-Step Update

The My Finances Home Page provides excellent information, but the quality of any information comes not just from its accuracy, but also from its timeliness. For example, it doesn't matter how accurate your investment portfolio is if you haven't updated your stock quotes since last year.

Quicken makes it easy to connect to the Internet and get the latest information with its One-Step Update feature. With a single click, you can update securities prices and news; download statements for checking, savings, credit card and investment accounts; and even download updates to Quicken itself, so you're always running the latest version of the program. Quicken automatically updates and reloads the data on the Home Page and in the Financial Centers.

To use One-Step Update:

1. Click the Online button in the global bar (**Figure 8.13**).

   or

   Select certain of the Actions (Get online quotes and news under the Watch List, for example) within the Activity Centers or the My Finances Home Page.

   or

   Select Finance > One Step Update.

   The One Step Update Download Selection window appears (**Figure 8.14**).

2. Click to select the items you want to update.

   Check marks will appear next to the items that you select. If you want to download financial statements for online-enabled accounts, you'll need to enter your PIN (Personal Identification Number) for those accounts.

3. Click Update Now.

   The Quicken 2000 Download Status screen (**Figure 8.15**) lets you know the progress of your update. If for some reason you want to halt the update process, you can click Stop Download.

4. The Download Summary window (**Figure 8.16**) appears when the update is complete. Review the information, and click on an underlined item to display the downloaded information.

   or

   Click Done.

Figure 8.13 The Online button is accessible from most Quicken windows.

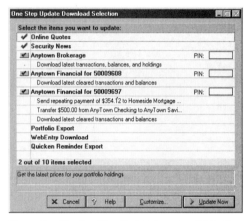

Figure 8.14 The One Step Update Download Selection window lets you control which information you want to download.

Figure 8.15 Downloading can take a while, depending on your modem speed, so the Download Status screen keeps you updated on what's happening.

Figure 8.16 After the update, Quicken lets you know what was downloaded and shows you any errors in this window.

USING ONE-STEP UPDATE

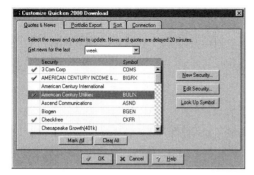

Figure 8.17 By selecting securities in this window, you can choose to update all or just a few of your security prices.

To customize which information you download:

1. Click the Online button in the global bar.

or

Choose Finance > One-Step Update.

The One Step Update Download Selection window appears (refer to Figure 8.14).

2. Click Customize.

The Customize Quicken 2000 Download window appears (**Figure 8.17**).

3. In the Quotes & News tab, choose the time period for the download from the "Get news for the last" drop-down list.

4. By default, all securities are already checked. Click on a security to toggle the check mark next to it on or off. You can also add or edit securities with the New Security and Edit security buttons. If you don't know the ticker symbol for a particular security, select it and click the Look Up Symbol button.

5. Click OK to save your changes.

Updating Quicken with One-Step Update

On occasion, Intuit updates Quicken to fix bugs or improve the program's performance. One-Step Update can let you know that an update is available, and can download the update program for you. After downloading, you'll need to exit Quicken and run the update program, after which you can pick up where you left off. All of your work is saved.

To update the Quicken program:

1. If an updated version of Quicken is available, the Download Summary will include a note at the bottom (**Figure 8.18**). Click Continue to download the update.

2. Click Update Now in the Update Available window (**Figure 8.19**).

   Quicken returns to the Internet to download the updater application (**Figure 8.20**).

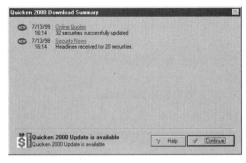

Figure 8.18 The Quicken 2000 Download Summary tells you that an update is available.

Figure 8.19 Click Update Now to begin downloading the update application.

Figure 8.20 Quicken downloads the application from its Internet site.

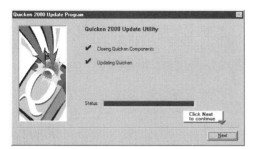

Figure 8.21 Click the Next button when the status bar is filled and the updater is ready for use.

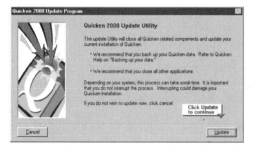

Figure 8.22 I recommend following Intuit's advice to shut down all open applications.

Figure 8.23 Congratulations! You have successfully updated your software!

3. Quicken checks your version of the program and prepares for the update. When the status bar is filled and the Next button is available (**Figure 8.21**), click it.

4. The next screen (**Figure 8.22**) tells you that the update could take some time (about 5 minutes or so, actually) and suggests that you close all other Windows applications. It's a good idea to do so.

5. Click Next.

   The next screen gives you a progress bar for the update; just wait until it's done.

6. The final updater screen (**Figure 8.23**) reports that all is well with the update, and lets you either finish the installation or go directly to Quicken. Either choice is fine.

BALANCING YOUR CHECKBOOK

9

Balancing your checkbook is one of Those Chores—things that everyone knows you need to do, that everyone says they do regularly, but that surprisingly few people actually do. And who can blame them? Balancing your checkbook by hand is a pain, especially if you have slacked off for a few months and need to catch up.

Tracking your checking account and balancing your checkbook is the number one reason why people buy Quicken. Quicken does a great job of reconciling accounts, and it makes a chore that took an hour to do by hand easy to finish in just a few minutes.

Quicken isn't limited to reconciling your checkbook, however. You can balance your savings, money market, or credit card accounts too. In addition to balancing accounts, you can update balances in cash, asset, or liability accounts to reflect transfers of funds, payments made, or interest received.

In this chapter, you'll learn how to reconcile accounts, update account balances, and resolve any differences between the bank's records and your own.

Balancing Accounts

You use the same procedure to balance a checking account, a savings account, or a money market account. First you enter your bank statement balance, and then you match transactions on your bank statement with transactions in your Quicken account register.

Balancing a credit card account works in almost the same way—except that if a balance is due on the credit card, Quicken will ask whether you want to make a payment at the end of the reconciliation process.

Before you begin, you should make sure that you have entered all transactions that occurred between the date of your last statement and the date of your current statement.

If you need to reconcile for more than one month, you'll first need to reconcile your account with the bank statements for each of the prior months before you try to reconcile the current month's statement.

To balance a checking, savings, or money market account:

1. Choose Banking > Bank Accounts > Account List, or press Ctrl A to open the Account List (**Figure 9.1**).

2. Double-click on the account that you wish to reconcile to open the account register (**Figure 9.2**).

3. Click the Reconcile button (which doesn't look like a button, even though it is) at the top of the register window (**Figure 9.3**). The Reconcile Bank Statement dialog box appears (**Figure 9.4**).

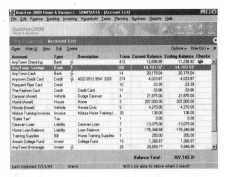

Figure 9.1 To begin reconciling, first open the register window.

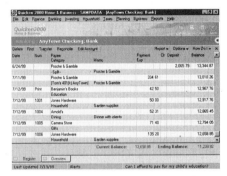

Figure 9.2 Select the account that you wish to reconcile from the scrolling list.

Figure 9.3 Click the Reconcile button to open the Reconcile Bank Statement dialog box.

Figure 9.4 Check to make sure that the beginning balance on your bank statement matches the amount in the "Opening Balance" field.

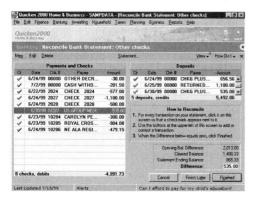

Figure 9.5 Click each transaction that has cleared on your bank statement in the Reconcile Bank Statement worksheet window.

4. Check to make sure that the beginning balance on your bank statement matches the amount in the Opening Balance box in the Reconcile Bank Statement dialog box. If the amounts don't match, click the Cancel button and fix the problem.

This problem can stem from a variety of causes, but it usually occurs because you haven't reconciled a previous month. See the Quicken user manual for details on fixing Opening Balance problems.

5. Enter the Ending Balance from your bank statement.

6. Enter the amount, date, and category of service charges or interest transactions.

7. Click the OK button.

The Reconcile Bank Statement worksheet window appears (**Figure 9.5**). This second window is where you do the real work of checking off each transaction in your register against your bank statement.

8. In the Clr column, Click each transaction that has cleared on your bank statement. A checkmark appears next to each cleared transaction.

9. Double-click any transaction in error in the Reconcile Bank Statement worksheet to open the account register and edit it.

or

To add a missing transaction, click the New button at the top of the window to open the account register and make the addition.

10. In either case, when you're done, click the Return to Reconcile button in the register to go back to the Reconcile Bank Statement worksheet window.

(continued)

11. As you check off each transaction, Quicken updates the Difference amount in the right lower corner of the Reconcile Bank Statement worksheet window. When you've checked off all the transactions, that figure should be zero If it is, click the Finished button.

12. If a difference amount still appears, skip to "Correcting Differences" later in this chapter to find out how to correct the problem.

13. If you balanced the account successfully, the Reconciliation Complete window appears (**Figure 9.6**). Quicken gives you the opportunity to create a reconciliation report. If you want the report, click the Yes button. Otherwise, click No.

✔ Tips

- At the top of the Reconcile Bank Statement worksheet window, the View dropdown list lets you sort items in the lists by check number, date, payee, or amount.

- If you want more room for deposit information in the Reconcile Bank Statement worksheet window, go to the View popup menu at the top of the window and uncheck "Show Instructions."

- You can get additional help on a variety of reconciliation topics by making a choice from the How Do I pop-up menu at the top of the Reconcile Bank Statement worksheet window (**Figure 9.7**).

- If your bank charges more than one service charge during the month, you can enter them added together in the Reconcile Bank Statement dialog box, or you can make separate entries in the register for each charge. Just make sure that you don't enter them twice.

Figure 9.6 If you want the report, click the Yes button. Otherwise, click No.

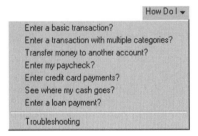

Figure 9.7 You can get more help with reconciling by choosing one of the topics under the How Do I pop-up menu.

Figure 9.8 After you balance the account successfully, the Make Credit Card Payment dialog box appears if you have an outstanding balance.

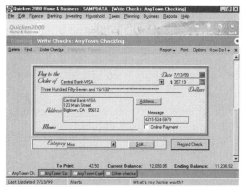

Figure 9.9 Click the Record Check button to make an entry in the register for payment to your credit card account.

To balance a credit card account:

1. Follow steps 1 through 11 above for a credit card account.

   You balance credit card accounts in almost the same way as checking, savings, or money market accounts.

2. If you reconcile successfully and you have an outstanding balance on your credit card, the Make Credit Card Payment dialog box appears (**Figure 9.8**).

3. If you want to make a payment on your credit card at this time, select the account you wish to use from the Bank Account drop-down list, and then select the means of payment using the Printed Check, Hand Written Check, or Online Payment radio buttons.

4. Click the Yes button.

   The Write Checks window appears (**Figure 9.9**).

5. Quicken writes the check for the entire amount of the outstanding balance. If you don't want to pay off the card at this time, edit the amount and fill in the rest of the check as you would normally (see Chapter 6 for more on writing checks).

6. Click the Record Check button.

   Quicken enters the payment in the register for the account you selected.

Correcting Differences

In the Reconcile window, if the Difference this Statement amount is not zero, it means that your account is not balancing for the current statement period. This usually occurs for one of two reasons: Either you've checked off a wrong number of payment or deposit items, or some of the checked items have incorrect dollar amounts.

To find the mistakes:

1. Count the number of credit items on your bank statement, and then count the number of deposits shown in the Reconcile window. If the number doesn't match, you've found the problem.

   or

   Compare the number of checks and payments on your bank statement against the number of debit items in the Reconcile Bank Statement window. You may have forgotten to record an item in the register, or you may have duplicated a transaction, entered a payment as a deposit or a deposit as a payment, or marked an item cleared by mistake.

2. If the number of items is correct but the statement still doesn't balance, you have a problem with the dollar amount of one or more of your items. By hand or using a calculator, add up all the transactions shown under Payments and Checks.

3. Compare this total with the total debits on the statement. If the numbers don't match, you have a problem with the dollar amount of the debits.

4. Add up all the transactions shown under Deposits and compare them to the total deposits on the statement. If those numbers don't match, there's a discrepancy in your deposit figures.

✔ Tips

■ The most common mistake in this area is transposing two digits during data entry.

■ If you're off by a fairly small amount that is a round number (for example, $8.00 rather than $3.87), it's likely that you missed entering a bank service charge of some sort. Check your statement carefully for charges you don't normally see, such as for check printing or using another bank's ATM.

■ Using Online Banking makes balancing your checkbook and other accounts even easier, because you download your bank and credit card statements directly into Quicken's account registers (see Chapter 10). And that downloading skips the data entry process—and any errors you might make.

Letting Quicken Fix the Problem

If the dollar amount of an unreconciled balance is small, you may decide that it's not worth the time it takes to track down the mistake. In that case, you can let Quicken enter a register adjustment, which will force your account to reconcile.

To let Quicken fix the problem:

1. If you clicked the Finished button in the Reconcile window even while a difference exists, Quicken will pop up the Adjust Register to Agree with Statement window (**Figure 9.10**).

2. To have Quicken to enter an account adjustment, click the Adjust button.

   or

   If you want to take another whack at finding the mistake, click Cancel.

✔ Tip

- Know when to quit. Unless you're the type who obsesses endlessly about that $2.53 you can't seem to account for, just let Quicken make the account adjustment. My rule of thumb is that if I can't balance after 15 minutes of trying, and the amount is under $20, I'll throw in the towel and make a balance adjustment. Adjust that rule to your own comfort level.

Figure 9.10 To have Quicken enter a balance adjustment for an account that just won't balance, click the Adjust button.

ONLINE BANKING AND BILL PAYING

Using your computer to download bank statements and pay bills is a new and, to some, scary way of dealing with your bank. Yet it can save you a lot of time and a bit of money.

Banking online saves you time spent recording your checks, ATM withdrawals, or credit card transactions by hand. Instead, you download them from your bank, review the transactions to catch any possible errors and make sure they are properly categorized, and then add them to your account registers with the click of a button. Because the information is current as of the close of the previous banking day, you can monitor your cash flow more closely. This lets you make sure, for example, that deposits are credited to your account before you write checks and helps you to avoid expensive bounced check charges. You can balance your checkbook in minutes every time you download your statement, instead of the much longer time it takes when working with a paper statement. Best of all, there's never any waiting in line when you're online.

Online bill payment lets you transfer money from your checking account directly to your creditors. You don't have to write or print checks, stuff envelopes, find stamps, or go to the post office. You simply enter a payment instruction in an account register and have Quicken send it over the phone lines to your bank, which then transfers the money.

Setting Up Online Banking

To use online banking, you must first set up access to the Internet (see Chapter 8 for information about getting Quicken connected to the Internet). Next, you'll have to apply for online banking, and then set up for online bill payment.

Applying for online banking

You must contact your bank or other financial institution to get online access for checking, savings, and credit card accounts. Not all financial institutions support online banking, and some support online banking only for certain account types, such as checking but not credit card accounts. Even if your financial institution doesn't support online banking, you can still use online bill payment through Intuit. If you have accounts at more than one financial institution, you'll need to apply to each one separately.

Each financial institution sets its own fees for online banking. The fee amount varies from bank to bank, so it's a good idea to shop around for the best deal. You can find a list of banks and their services and fees on Intuit's Web site by choosing Finance > Online Financial Institutions List. You'll find out if your bank has online access available, and if it does, the phone number or email address to contact to get the application process started (**Figure 10.1**). Some banks provide an Apply Now button that lets you sign up on the spot. You can also find a list of participating institutions as part of the Online Banking Setup, although the list on the Web site is kept up to date and is obviously more complete.

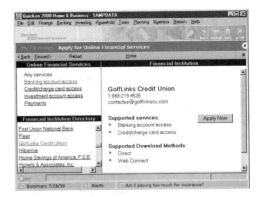

Figure 10.1 To see if your bank offers online access, check the list on Intuit's Web site.

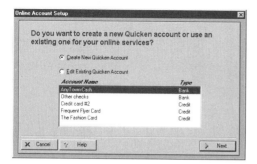

Figure 10.2 Begin the online access process in the Online Account Setup window.

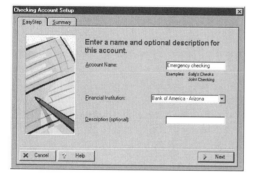

Figure 10.3 Select an account name and the financial institution you'll be using for online service.

After you have signed up for online banking, your financial institution will send you a kit with the information that you'll need to set up your Quicken accounts for online banking. You'll also receive an initial personal identification number (PIN), which you should change in your first online banking session.

To create a new Quicken account for online use:

1. Choose Banking > Online Banking Setup. The Online Account Setup window appears (**Figure 10.2**).

2. Click the Create New Quicken Account radio button to create a new account. Click Next.

   The Account Setup screen appears (**Figure 10.3**).

3. Name the account and then choose a financial institution from the drop-down list. If your bank's name does not appear, you can type it in, but you will not be able to access it directly through Quicken. Click Next.

4. Proceed with the account setup process as explained back in Chapter 2. In the Online information area of the Summary window, choose the "Account Access" and "Online Payment" options you need. One or the other or both may be available, depending on the institution you have selected.

   If you have not chosen an institution and you select "Enable Online Payment," Quicken will choose "Intuit Online Payment" as your financial institution by default. Click Next.

5. On the Edit Bank Account screen, enter the routing number you have received from the bank for the account. Click Next.

   (continued)

SETTING UP ONLINE BANKING

6. On the next screen, enter the account number and type. Click Next.

7. Enter the Customer ID you received from the institution.

8. On the summary screens, check that everything's OK and then click Done.

9. A Service Agreement Information box appears. Read the small print if you feel compelled to, and then click OK. Your account is now set up.

10. Once the account is set up, choose Banking > Online Banking.

    Quicken will connect with your financial institution to download your account information.

✔ Tip

■ If you leave the financial institution field blank, Quicken will offer you an alphabetical list of banks with the services they offer and contact information. You may make your selection there and continue with the process of enabling online banking.

SETTING UP ONLINE BANKING

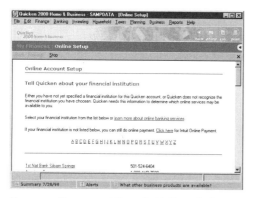

Figure 10.4 You can sort through this list to find an institution to your liking.

To use an existing account for online banking:

1. Choose Banking > Online Banking Setup. The Online Account Setup window appears. (Refer to **Figure 10.2.**)

2. Click the Edit Existing Quicken Account radio button and highlight the one you want to use in the "Account Name" list. Click Next.

    If the account you have chosen is not with a bank Quicken recognizes, an Online Setup screen appears (**Figure 10.4**) with information about a number of banks you can use. Alternatively, you can use Intuit's own online payment system.

3. If your account is with a Quicken recognized institution, you'll see an Online Setup window with a three-step procedure to get you on your way to Internet access. Complete these three steps and you'll be ready to enjoy all the benefits of online banking.

4. After your account is set up, choose Banking > Online Banking.

    Quicken will connect with your financial institution to download your account information.

SETTING UP ONLINE BANKING

Going Online

The first time that you go online, it's a good idea to download your current transactions. This gets you used to the process and lets you update your account registers. During this first session, your bank may prompt you to change your PIN, which results in even better security.

To download transactions:

1. Switch to the online banking area (**Figure 10.5**) by choosing Banking > Online Banking.

2. If you have online accounts at more than one financial institution, choose the institution from the Financial Institution drop-down list. Then click the Update/Send button. The Instructions to Send window appears (**Figure 10.6**).

3. Enter your PIN, and then click the Send button.

4. The Quicken 2000 Download Summary window appears (**Figure 10.7**). Review the information, and then click the Done button.

5. Quicken displays the downloaded transactions in the bottom half of the Online Center window (**Figure 10.8**). Click the Compare to Register button, which opens up the register for that account, with the downloaded transactions below (**Figure 10.9**).

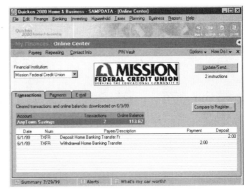

Figure 10.5 You'll begin downloading transactions in this window.

Figure 10.6 You tell Quicken what online actions to take in this window.

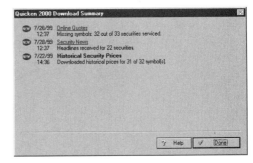

Figure 10.7 Review the information in the Download Summary window, and then click OK.

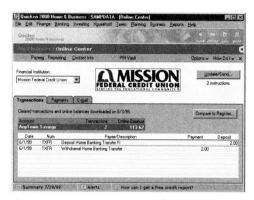

Figure 10.8 Switch between newly downloaded transactions in your various accounts by selecting the account name.

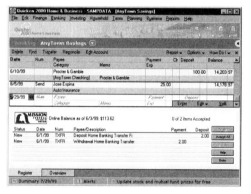

Figure 10.9 Compare the downloaded transactions with your register items, and add payee or category information as needed.

6. Quicken compares the downloaded transactions with those that are already in your account register. If the transactions correspond, the word "Match" appears in the Status column next to the downloaded transaction. Select each matched transaction, then click the Accept button, signifying that you're ready to clear it in your register. Quicken changes the status from Match to Accepted.

If Quicken doesn't find a match for a downloaded transaction, it marks the transaction as New in the Status column. Quicken marks a transaction as New when you haven't yet entered that transaction in your account register or when the check number or amount differs from the transaction that you entered.

7. For these New transactions, you'll need to enter the missing payee and/or category information. Select the New item in the transaction list, and Quicken displays the transaction in the register.

8. Make your changes in the register, and then click the Enter button. The transaction's status changes to Match. Click the Accept button.

9. Repeat steps 7 and 8 for every new transaction.

10. Click the Done button.

   Quicken adds the Accepted items to the account register, marking them as cleared, and removes them from the transaction list in the Online Center.

(continued)

GOING ONLINE

✔ Tips

- Your financial institution may label ATM transactions and service charges as EFT, which stands for Electronic Funds Transfer.

- Quicken doesn't automatically close the Internet connection after it finishes downloading, so if you're using a dial-up connection, you must close it manually.

- Headings in the Download Summary window that look like hyperlinks really are; you can click on them to go immediately to downloaded information.

Is Online Banking Secure?

Since online banking and online bill payment transactions travel over the Internet, it's perfectly reasonable to wonder if criminals can intercept and use your financial data. Quicken's security measures make it extremely unlikely.

The first line of defense is the Personal Identification Number (PIN) that you must enter whenever you use online banking or bill payment. When you first sign up for online banking, your bank sends you a PIN that you can (and should) change. After you change it, you're the only one who knows that PIN. For extra security, you should change your PIN on a regular basis.

For additional security, Quicken encrypts all transferred information—back and forth. Encryption is a technique that uses a mathematical algorithm to scramble data before it is sent. At the other end, your bank unscrambles the data. (The more technically inclined may be interested to know that Quicken uses 128-bit DES [Data Encryption Standard] encryption along with SSL [Secure Sockets Layer] transfer protocols.)

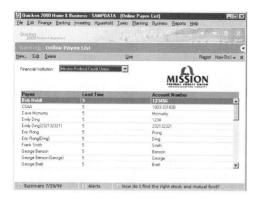

Figure 10.10 The Online Payee List window shows the people and companies you've set up for online payments, and how much lead time they need to accept payment.

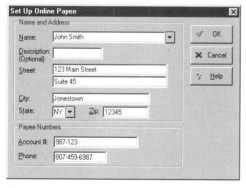

Figure 10.11 Enter the payee's information and account number in the Set Up Online Payee window.

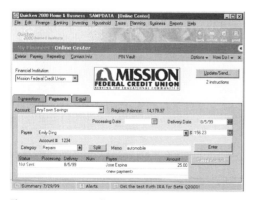

Figure 10.12 Enter online payments in the Payments tab of the Online Center window.

Paying Bills Online

To make online bill payments with Quicken, you'll first need to set up the payment recipients in the Payee list. To send a payment, you just select a payee from the list, create the payment instruction, and send it to your financial institution.

To set up a payee:

1. Choose Banking > Online Payee List.
   The Online Payee List window appears (**Figure 10.10**).

2. Click the New button at the top left of the window to open the Set Up Online Payee window (**Figure 10.11**).

3. Enter the payee's name, address, and phone number.

4. Enter the account number that the payee uses to identify you. If the payee doesn't use account numbers, enter your name.

5. Click the OK button. Quicken presents a dialog box asking you to review and verify the payee information. If all is correct, click the Accept button; otherwise, click the Cancel button and correct the payee information.

   After you verify the information, Quicken adds the new payee to the Payee list.

To create and send an online payment:

1. Choose Banking > Online Payee List. The Online Payee List appears.

2. Select one of the payees, and then click the Use button. The Online Center window opens, and the payee's name and account information transfers to the Payments tab of that window (**Figure 10.12**).

3. Fill in the amount and the category in the Payments tab.

(continued)

4. If you plan to create more online payments in the current session, click the Enter button. Quicken stores the payment in a list of instructions to send to your financial institution the next time you connect. If this is the only payment you are making, click the Update/Send button. Quicken immediately connects online, prompts you for your PIN, and sends your payment instruction.

5. When you're done adding online payments, click the Update/Send button to open the Instructions to Send window (refer to **Figure 10.6**).

6. Review the items, and if you're satisfied, click the Send button. Quicken connects to your financial institution and sends the payments.

✔ Tips

■ If your payee is set up to receive electronic funds transfers, payment transfers directly from your account to your payee's account. This usually takes less than two business days. If the payee doesn't accept EFTs, your financial institution prints a check and sends it to the payee by U.S. mail. It's important that you allow sufficient time for the payment to get to the payee to avoid a late charge. So make sure that you schedule payments at least three or four days before their due date.

■ Don't forget that a payee often needs a day or two after receiving a check to process the payment and credit your account.

PAYING BILLS ONLINE

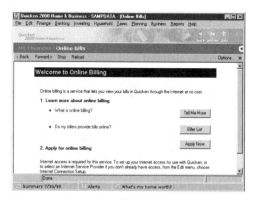

Figure 10.13 The Online Bills screen gets you started on your way toward a paperless financial future.

Using Online Billing

With Quicken 2000, Intuit is introducing Online Billing, the natural companion to Online Payment. Once this new system gets up and running—and it is only in its infancy now—you will be able to receive your bills over the Internet, automatically enter them into your account register, and then turn around and pay them online. No paper, no stamps, and no charge for this service. You can even have Intuit notify you by email when you have a new bill. As of the summer of 1999, when I wrote this, only a small number of billers were set up to be able to present their bills this way. These companies included Amoco, BellSouth, MCI Worldcom, and Boston Edison. Many others are expected to join the program in the near future.

To set up Online Billing:

◆ Choose Banking > Online Billing.

The Online Bills screen (**Figure 10.13**) opens with information about the system, participating vendors, and a link to the Internet site where you can apply for the service. To get a complete explanation of the Online Billing process, click the Tell Me More button. To find out if any of your billers are currently participating, click the Biller List button. And to apply to use online billing, click the Apply Now button.

DEALING WITH CREDIT CARDS

Credit cards are an incredibly convenient way to make purchases. They make it easy to buy things now and pay for them later. The price you pay for this convenience, of course, is the interest your credit card company charges as compensation for the loan of their money. And as purchases and interest charges mount, it's all too easy to get to the point where your credit card debt becomes overwhelming.

If you're already at the point where you are uncomfortable with the size of your debt load, you should use Quicken's Debt Reduction Planner to develop a plan to get out of debt. See Chapter 19 for more about the Debt Reduction Planner.

One way to make sure that your credit card debt doesn't spin out of control is to track it carefully on a monthly basis. That means categorizing your card charges so that you know where you're spending your money, and reconciling your credit card accounts to make sure that spending doesn't slip by unnoticed.

It's also a good idea to take advantage of Quicken's built-in tools that let you know if you spend more than you want to in a particular category, help you find the best credit card rate, and help you set account limits.

Tracking Credit Card Transactions

There are two main methods for tracking credit card transactions within Quicken. The first method is to use a credit card account with an associated register to track each and every transaction separately (**Figure 11.1**). This method lets you see all the transactions within the credit card account, including the current balance; you can create more comprehensive reports about your spending; and it's easier to find and correct data entry errors. However, it does require a little more data entry (although if you arrange to download your credit card statement over the Internet, there's almost no data entry at all).

The other way to handle your credit card transactions is if you always pay your bill in full each month. You would enter the credit card payment into your checking account register, creating a split transaction with a separate line for each purchase you made this month (**Figure 11.2**). This method saves a little bit of data entry, and keeps all of your transactions within your checking account. You have to be a little cleverer about selecting reports to display your spending, and if you run a balance, you won't be able to track that balance in Quicken; you'll need to refer to your paper statement. You also won't have any easy way to track credits to your credit card account.

Personally, I favor the first method of tracking. Sure, it's a bit more data entry, but if I do happen to run a balance for a particular month, I know just what that balance is. And it's much simpler to see where my purchases occurred without having to go into my check register and open each split transaction. Pick a method based on your spending and payment habits, and on the importance of debt tracking in your situation.

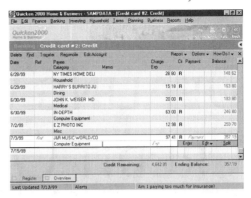

Figure 11.1 The best way to handle credit card transactions is to make all your entries in a separate credit card account.

Figure 11.2 Another way to track credit cards is to make payments in your check register, creating split transactions to track the categories for your charges.

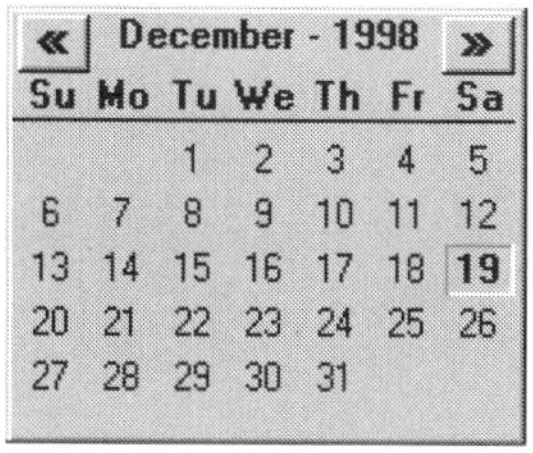

Figure 11.3 This pop-up calendar makes it easy to select a transaction date.

Figure 11.4 You enter both charges and payments in the credit card register.

To enter a credit card transaction in a credit card account:

1. Choose Banking > Bank Accounts, and then choose your credit card account from the list.

2. The credit card account register appears (refer to **Figure 11.1**) with the current date filled in and the Date field highlighted. You can change the date by typing in a new date, or by clicking the calendar icon underneath the date (**Figure 11.3**).

3. Press the ⌧Tab⌧ key to move to the Ref field. This is usually unused in a credit card account (you might see a reference number entered here if you download your credit card statement), so press ⌧Tab⌧ again to get to the Payee field.

4. Enter the payee (for a charge) or the name of your credit card company (for a payment).

5. Enter the charge or payment amount.

6. Assign a category to the transaction by typing it into the Category field. The QuickFill feature fills in the category name from the pop-up menu after you enter the first few letters. You can also use the pop-up menu in the Category field to select the category.

7. Enter a memo about the transaction (optional).

8. Click the Enter button (or press the ⌧Enter⌧ key on the keyboard). Quicken saves the transaction and adds it to the register (**Figure 11.4**).

TRACKING CREDIT CARD TRANSACTIONS

To enter a credit card transaction in a checking account register:

1. Open a checking account register.

2. Enter the date, the check number, the name of your credit card company, and the total payment amount.

3. Click the Split button in the register. The Split Transaction window appears. You'll enter each charge to your account in the split lines.

4. Enter the category for the first charge in the first Category field in the split, either by typing the category in or by choosing it from the pop-up menu.

5. Type the name of the store or merchant in the first Memo field. If needed, also enter a description of the charge here.

6. Type the amount of the charge in the first Amount field. Quicken subtracts that amount from the total and puts the remainder in the next Amount field.

7. Enter the next category, merchant, and amount on the next line. Repeat this until you have allocated the entire payment or deposit amount and there is zero Remainder in the summary at the bottom of the window (refer to **Figure 11.2**).

8. Click the OK button to save the transaction, properly allocated to multiple categories.

Figure 11.5 Start setting credit card limits in the Account List.

Figure 11.6 Update your credit card limit in this window.

Controlling Credit Card Debt

Quicken can't keep you from using your credit cards, but it can let you know when your spending goes over a specified amount. Quicken can alert you when you've hit your credit limit, or when you've spent more than you can comfortably pay off in a month. If you have problems with spending in one or two areas (for example, if you just can't stop buying clothes or books), you can set an alert for one or more categories.

Finally, one way to control your credit card debt is not to spend as much for debt service. That means using Quicken.com to find the best interest rates on credit cards; there's no reason to spend more money than necessary on interest. See Chapter 20 for more information on using Quicken.com.

To enter your credit limit for a credit card account:

1. Choose Banking > Bank Accounts > Account List or press Ctrl A. The Account List opens (**Figure 11.5**).

2. Click a credit card account to select it.

3. At the top of the Account List, click the Edit button. The Overview window for that account appears (**Figure 11.6**).

4. Enter the credit limit, and then either click the x in the upper-right corner to exit the account or click the Register tab at the bottom to return to the register.

Or

1. Open the credit card register.

2. Click the Overview tab at the bottom of the register.

3. Make whatever changes you need, and exit either back to the register or to somewhere else in the program.

To set a spending alert for a credit card account:

1. Click the Alerts box in the Status bar at the bottom of the Quicken window, or choose Finance > Alerts. The Set Up Alerts window appears.

2. Click the Accounts tab, then under Select an account alert, choose Credit Card Limits (**Figure 11.7**). The window changes to display your credit card accounts on the right side of the window.

3. For each credit card, enter a figure in the Remind Me At field. I suggest you enter a number no higher than you feel you can comfortably pay off in one month. Also make sure that the *total* of all the amounts in the Remind Me At fields isn't more than you can handle each month.

4. Click OK to save your changes. After you set up these alerts, Quicken Home Page will let you know when you get dangerously close to your credit limits (**Figure 11.8**).

To set alerts on specific spending categories:

1. Click the Alerts box in the Status bar at the bottom of the Quicken window, or choose Finance > Alerts. The Set Up Alerts window appears.

2. Click the Accounts tab, then under Select an account alert, choose Monthly Expenses. The window changes to display your spending categories on the right side of the window.

3. Scroll through the list, entering amounts as necessary in the Spending Limit fields (**Figure 11.9**).

4. Click OK to save your changes.

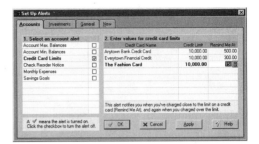

Figure 11.7 You'll get a warning before you get into financial trouble if you set your reminder amounts low.

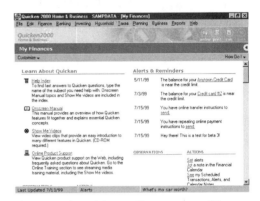

Figure 11.8 The Quicken My Finances page will let you know when you are skating close to your credit card limits.

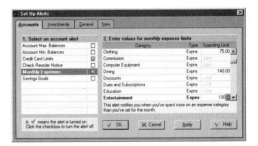

Figure 11.9 Worried that you spend too much on shoes each month? Set up category limits, and Quicken will let you know that it's time to skip your next pair.

WORKING WITH LOANS AND MORTGAGES

Loans come in two flavors: Either you are borrowing money from another person or from a financial institution, or, perhaps a happier situation, you are lending money to someone else. Quicken handles both kinds of loans with aplomb, creating an account for each new loan.

When you are borrowing money, Quicken tracks how the loan is *amortized*, or paid off, to show you the interest you are paying, the remaining principal, and the length and amounts of your payment schedule. When you set up this kind of loan, Quicken automatically creates a *liability* account.

When you loan money to someone else, Quicken sets up a payment schedule and creates an *asset* account.

Creating Loans

To set up a loan account, Quicken needs information about the terms of the loan and the lender or borrower. Then Quicken creates the loan payment schedule and the principal asset or liability account.

To create a loan (when you're the borrower):

1. Choose Household > Loans, or press Ctrl H. The View Loans window appears (**Figure 12.1**). If you already have an existing loan, the window will show the loan's summary.

2. Click the New button at the top of the window. The Loan Setup window appears (**Figure 12.2**). Click the Next button.

3. Select the Borrow Money radio button in the "What type of loan is this?" screen, then click the Next button.

4. The "Choose a Quicken account for this loan" screen allows you to enter the name of the new liability account for the loan, or if you had already set up a liability account, allows you to select it. Click Next.

5. The next screen asks if you have made any payments on the loan. Click the Yes or No button, then click Next.

6. Enter the Opening Date and the Original Balance for the loan, then click Next.

7. Click Yes if there will be a balloon payment at the end of the loan, otherwise click No and then Next.

8. Enter the loan length, then click Next.

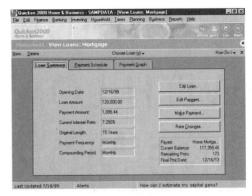

Figure 12.1 The View Loans window shows the loans you've entered and lets you start a new loan account.

Figure 12.2 In the Loan Setup window, Quicken learns about the kind of loan that you want to set up.

Figure 12.3 Check over the information you entered in the Summary screens.

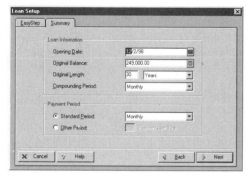

Figure 12.4 Quicken confirms the rest of the information you entered.

Figure 12.5 You can schedule the loan payment from the Set Up Loan Payment window.

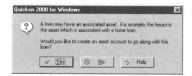

Figure 12.6 You'll get a chance to set up an associated asset account for your loan.

9. Indicate the frequency of the payment. If you will pay on a schedule other than monthly (the default), change the setting of the Frequency drop-down list.

10. Enter the compounding period, which is how often the amount of interest owed is recalculated. It's usually monthly.

11. Enter the date of your first payment.

12. If you know the amount of the first payment, click Yes; otherwise, Quicken will calculate it for you.

13. Enter the annual interest rate. If you're entering an adjustable-rate loan, use the rate that is applied to the first payment.

14. The first Summary screen appears (**Figure 12.3**). Check that the information is correct, then click Next.

15. Review the information on the second Summary screen (**Figure 12.4**), correcting any errors. Do the same for the next Summary screen, then click Done. The Set Up Loan Payment screen appears (**Figure 12.5**).

16. Enter any information still needed (the payee name, for example) in the Set Up Loan Payment window, then click OK.

17. To make this loan payment a Scheduled Transaction, click the Payment Method button, then click Scheduled Transaction and set appropriate options (see Chapter 5 for more on scheduled transactions).

18. If you're creating a loan for a mortgage, Quicken asks if you want to create an associated asset account, since your home is an asset, just as the mortgage is a liability (see **Figure 12.6**). Click Yes or No. You'll return to the View Loans window.

(continued)

✔ Tips

- The term of a loan must be at least 12 months for Quicken to be able to calculate the interest, principal, and payment information.

- For variable-rate loans, you can change the interest rate when you make a payment or whenever your loan's interest rate changes.

- In the Preview Payment window, the principal and interest amount applies to the next scheduled payment only. That's because Quicken calculates the correct amounts for these numbers every time that you make a payment.

- You can specify whether you want to pay your loan with a handwritten check, an online banking transaction, or a printed check by selecting the appropriate radio button in the Set Up Loan Payment window.

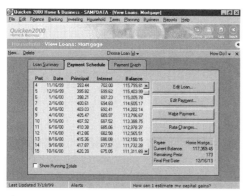

Figure 12.7 You can review the payment schedule for any loan by clicking the Payment Schedule tab in the View Loans window.

To view your payment schedule:

1. Choose Household > Loans, or press Ctrl H. The View Loans window appears (refer to **Figure 12.1**).

2. If necessary, change the loan you're displaying with the Choose Loan menu.

3. Click the Payment Schedule tab in the View Loans window. The Payment Schedule for that loan appears (**Figure 12.7**).

To create a loan (when you're lending):

1. Choose Household > Loans, or press Ctrl H. The View Loans window appears (refer to **Figure 12.1**). If you already have an existing loan, the window will show the loan's summary.

2. Click the New button at the top of the window. The Loan Setup window appears (refer to **Figure 12.2**). Click the Next button. Click the New button. The Loan Interview window appears.

3. Select the Lend Money radio button and any others that are appropriate for this loan and then click the Next button. Fill out the rest of the information in the Loan Setup and Loan Payment Setup windows.

Making Loan Payments

To make a loan payment, you first recall the loan payment from the Loans list and then make the payment. Quicken calculates the principal and interest amounts and updates the loan balance.

Of course, you don't have to do this manually if you have a fixed-rate loan. It's easy to schedule the loan payment for automatic entry using the Calendar (as discussed in Chapter 7).

To make a loan payment:

1. Choose Household > Loans, or press ⟨Ctrl⟩⟨H⟩. The View Loans window appears (refer to **Figure 12.1**). If you already have an existing loan, the window will show the loan's summary.

2. Select the loan for which you want to enter a payment using the Choose Loan menu. Then click the Make Payment button. The Loan Payment dialog box appears (**Figure 12.8**). If this is a regular payment, click the Regular button. The Make Regular Payment window appears (**Figure 12.9**). If instead you're making an extra payment, click the Extra button.

3. If you need to make any adjustments in the Payment window, enter them now.

4. Click the OK button. Quicken will enter the loan payment in the account register.

✔ Tip

■ To see the history of a loan, open the account register for the loan from the Accounts list. Your register should resemble **Figure 12.10**.

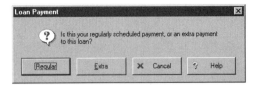

Figure 12.8 You can choose to make a regular or extra payment in the Loan Payment dialog box.

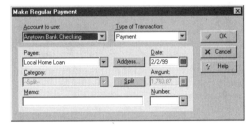

Figure 12.9 Make any changes to your payment information in the Make Regular Payment window.

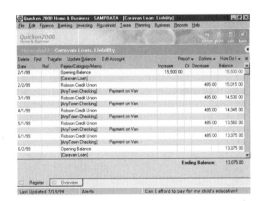

Figure 12.10 Like all Quicken accounts, loans have their own register windows.

QUICKEN AT TAX TIME

Maybe some people enjoy paying taxes, but personally I've never met them. For most of us, preparing and paying taxes is a yearly ritual that we could easily live without.

Quicken can help ease some of the pain (nothing relieves the agony of writing a check instead of receiving a refund). If you properly categorize your income and expenses through the year, you'll be able to create reports that make filling out your tax forms much easier. These reports can also save you money if someone else does your taxes, because the preparer will have less digging to do to get a clear picture of your finances.

Do-it-yourself types can transfer Quicken data to a tax preparation program called TurboTax, also made by Intuit. With federal and state tax forms built in, TurboTax can do a complete job of tax preparation, from helping you find information to calculating and printing your final tax return. If you prefer to use other tax preparation programs, you can export your Quicken data for their use. When it comes to taxes, I hate surprises. I use the Quicken Tax Planner to get a ballpark figure for my taxes before I see my accountant.

In this chapter, you'll see how to set Quicken up for taxes, do some tax planning, create tax reports, and get your Quicken data ready for a tax preparation program.

Linking Categories to Federal Tax Forms

When you set up your Quicken categories, you may have linked the categories that you customized with particular federal tax forms (see "Using Tax Links" in Chapter 3). Quicken gives you another way to set up tax links that's more comprehensive than the technique shown in Chapter 3.

To connect categories with lines on tax forms:

1. Choose Finance > Category & Transfer List. The Category & Transfer List opens (**Figure 13.1**).

2. From the Options menu at the top of the Category & Transfer List window, choose Assign Tax Items (**Figure 13.2**). The Tax Link Assistant appears (**Figure 13.3**).

3. Under the Category column, scroll through the list until you find the first of the categories that you wish to link to a line on a federal tax form. Then click once on the category name to select it.

4. Under the Tax Form Line Items column, scroll the list until you find the appropriate line item for the category you selected. Then click on the line item, selecting it. Note that when you select a line item, descriptive text about the line item appears at the bottom of the Tax Link Assistant window (**Figure 13.4**).

5. Click the Assign Line Item to Category button.

6. Repeat steps 3 to 5 as needed with other categories. When you're finished, click the OK button to save your changes.

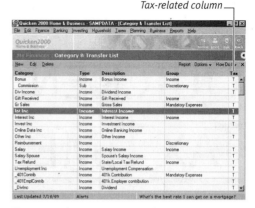

Tax-related column

Figure 13.1 The Category & Transfer List shows which categories are tax related.

Figure 13.2 Choose Assign Tax Items to begin the tax linking process.

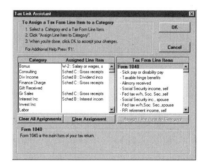

Figure 13.3 The Tax Link Assistant.

Figure 13.4 You can make sure that you're assigning categories correctly with the Tax Link Assistant.

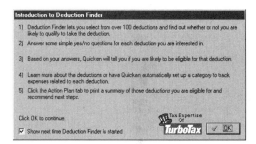

Figure 13.5 Read this introductory screen for information about deductions.

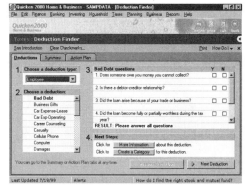

Figure 13.6 The Deduction Finder can help you zero in on deductions—and save you money.

Figure 13.7 Choose a deduction category to determine potential tax deductions.

Planning for Taxes

You can't avoid paying taxes altogether, but it's perfectly OK to work hard at finding and using every tax deduction that you can legally claim. Quicken has two tools that you can use to help reduce your tax load: the Tax Deduction Finder, which sniffs out deductions you may not have considered, and the Quicken Tax Planner, a financial calculator that lets you try out different tax scenarios.

To use the Tax Deduction Finder:

1. Choose Taxes > Deduction Finder. The Tax Deduction Finder window opens and the introduction screen appears (**Figure 13.5**).

2. Read the introductory information. Then click the OK button. The Deduction Finder screen appears, set to the Deductions tab (**Figure 13.6**).

3. From the Choose a deduction type drop-down list, pick the category of deduction you want to explore (**Figure 13.7**).

4. The Tax Deduction Finder tests to determine whether you qualify for a particular deduction by asking you a series of questions about each deduction. Select a deduction from the scrolling list on the left side of the screen. On the right side, click Yes or No to answer each question. Once you answer all the questions for that deduction, the planner will tell you either that you can't take the deduction or that you may be eligible for it.

(continued)

5. If you possibly qualify for the deduction, you can take one of two actions in the Next Steps section of the window. Clicking the More Information button opens a window with detailed information about the deduction (**Figure 13.8**). Review the information, then click the OK button to return to the Deduction Finder. You can also click the Create a Category button to add a category covering the deduction to your Quicken data file. The Create a category window appears, summarizing the category information (**Figure 13.9**). Click the OK button to add the category. If you don't want to add the category, click the Cancel button.

6. Continue choosing deductions in the scrolling list on the left side of the screen until you have worked through all the deductions that you think may apply to you. Then choose one of the other types under Choose a deduction type to show the deductions for that type.

7. When you have worked through all of the areas under Choose a deduction type, click the Summary tab. The Summary screen appears (**Figure 13.10**), listing your deduction categories.

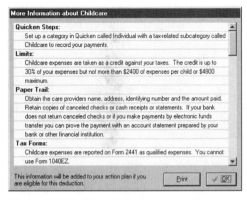

Figure 13.8 You will get all the information you need about a deduction in the More Information screen.

Figure 13.9 Click OK to add a deduction category to your Quicken data file.

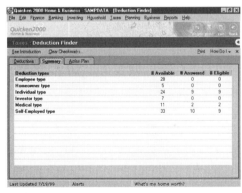

Figure 13.10 This screen offers a summary of your tax deductions.

PLANNING FOR TAXES

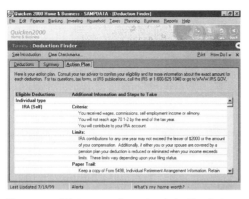

Figure 13.11 Print a copy of your tax deduction Action Plan for your accountant from this screen.

8. Review the Summary screen, and then click the Action Plan tab. The Action Plan screen appears (**Figure 13.11**).

9. If you want a copy of your Action Plan to show to your tax preparer, click the Print button at the top of the Deduction Finder screen.

✔ Tip

■ The Tax Deduction Finder uses internal information based on the 1998 tax year. Since the tax code changes every year, you'll want to make sure that you check over the recommendations in your Action Plan with your accountant or with another tax professional. Or you can call the Internal Revenue Service with general tax questions at (800) 829-1040, or go to its Web site at http://www.irs.gov.

PLANNING FOR TAXES

To use the Tax Planner:

1. Choose Taxes > Tax Planner. The Tax Planner window appears (**Figure 13.12**).

2. Under Filing Status and Tax Year at the top of the window, choose your filing status and the tax year from the pop-up menus.

3. Click the Quicken Data button at the top of the window to have the planner import your financial data from your data file. The Preview Quicken Tax Data window opens (**Figure 13.13**).

4. If your data is for less than an entire year, you can annualize individual categories, allowing you to estimate the value of that category for a whole year. Double-click a line to toggle it between annualized and year-to-date amounts. You can also use the Annualize None or Annualize All buttons to speed the process. Click the OK button to return to the Tax Planner, which now contains the imported data.

5. You can click any of the buttons in the Income or Tax Computation areas to enter detailed information.

6. After all your tax information is entered, the tax planner calculates your total tax, which shows you the amount you owe the IRS or the amount of your refund.

✔ Tip

- If you want to see the tax implications of decisions such as buying a home or filing taxes jointly or separately, you can try out three different tax scenarios, and Quicken will give you the results. Click the Scenarios button, fill in the Alternate Case information, and then click the Compare button to see a summary screen of how each scenario turns out (**Figure 13.14**).

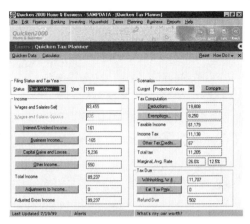

Figure 13.12 In the Tax Planner window, click the Quicken Data button and Quicken will insert your preentered data.

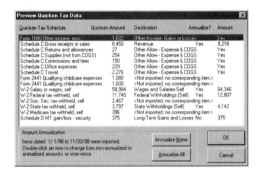

Figure 13.13 You get a chance to annualize your imported data in the Preview Quicken Tax Data window.

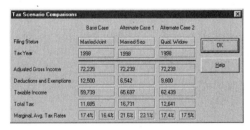

Figure 13.14 This summary of different tax scenarios shows you clearly which choice will save you money.

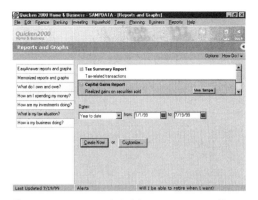

Figure 13.15 You can ask Quicken to create specific tax reports from this window.

Export button

Figure 13.16 The Tax Schedule report is only one of three types of tax reports you can export to specialized tax preparation programs.

Creating Tax Reports

Your accountant will probably be interested in three kinds of Quicken reports for preparing your tax return:

◆ A Tax Summary report shows your tax-related income and expenses, subtotaled by category.

◆ The Tax Schedule report groups information from all accounts in your data file that have tax lines assigned to them. The report lists information grouped by tax form.

◆ A Capital Gains report shows the realized capital gains from your investment accounts.

You create and print all of these reports in almost exactly the same way. (For more information about creating reports, see Chapter 17.)

To create a tax report:

1. Choose Reports > Reports and Graphs Center, and then select the "What is my tax situation?" tab (**Figure 13.15**).

2. Click on Tax Summary, Capital Gains, or Tax Schedule in the window.

3. Choose the date range in the window and customize the report as needed.

4. Click the Create button. Quicken creates and displays the report you selected (**Figure 13.16**).

Exporting Quicken Data

Quicken can save data from a Tax Schedule report or a Capital Gains report in a standard format that's compatible with many tax preparation programs. This format is called Tax Exchange Format (TXF). The tax program can then read the TXF file, saving you a lot of repetitive data entry. If you choose to use TurboTax, which Intuit also makes, you won't have to export your file—TurboTax can find and use your Quicken data directly.

To export Quicken data:

1. Create a Tax Schedule or Capital Gains report, and leave it open on your screen.

2. Click the Export button at the top of the report window. The Create Tax Export File dialog box will appear (**Figure 13.17**).

3. Enter a name for the report file in the File name box.

4. Choose Tax export files (TXF) from the Files of type drop-down list.

5. Click the OK button.

To use Quicken data in TurboTax:

◆ Choose Taxes > Web Turbo Tax.

A new window opens, welcoming you to WebTurboTax, where you can prepare your federal and local taxes online.

Figure 13.17 In this dialog box, you can save the exported tax data file.

EXPORTING QUICKEN DATA

PART 2

INVESTING

Setting Up Investment Accounts

When you're in your twenties, retirement seems a lifetime away, but ironically, that's just when you should begin investing, because you'll have nearly 50 years for your interest to compound. Professional financial planners like to show how if you save just $100 per month starting when you're 20, you can easily retire with savings of more than a million dollars. Make the same investments starting at 30, and at 65 you have only about a third as much. If you're already past your twenties and thirties, don't despair—it's never too late to start preparing for your future.

For most of us, the key to a successful retirement is a solid and consistent savings and investment program. Given the general trend toward an older population, and uncertainties about the ability of Social Security to handle the expected load of retirees in the 21st century, it's wise to supplement pension programs from your job or the government with your own investment plan. Quicken lets you track the performance of your investments, update current market values, and see whether you're earning or losing money on your investments.

In this chapter, you'll learn how to set up an investment portfolio, how to add investments to your portfolio, and how to set up a mutual fund account in Quicken.

Using Investment Accounts

You can use a variety of account types within Quicken to track your investments. Here are the choices:

◆ Use a **regular bank account** for investments with a constant share price or no share price. For example, a certificate of deposit (CD) earns interest, but the value doesn't go up or down according to a fluctuating market.

◆ Use **asset accounts** to keep track of things that you own, such as personal property, real estate, or other tangible items. For example, if you have a valuable stamp or wine collection, you might track its value in an asset account so that the collection shows up as part of your net worth. You can update the value of the collection in the asset account from time to time.

One drawback of using a bank account or an asset account is that it cannot track the rate of return on an investment. To track a return rate, you'll need to use one of these types of accounts:

◆ A **Brokerage account** tracks one or more securities. (A security is an investment vehicle, such as a stock, bond, mutual fund, money-market fund, certificate of deposit, precious metal, or collectible.) Your Brokerage account can include a mix of securities, and you can use the account to track transactions and provide the total market value for your portfolio. Quicken's many reporting options can show you how your portfolio is performing.

◆ A **special kind of Brokerage account** tracks a single mutual fund. (Of course, you can have as many single mutual fund accounts as you wish, each tracking a different mutual fund.)

It's a good idea to have accounts in Quicken that correspond to your real-world accounts. For example, if the extent of your investments is that you own a single mutual fund, just create one single mutual fund account to match. But if you have an account with a broker who maintains a portfolio for you—which can be a mix of stocks, bonds, mutual funds, cash, and other securities—then you'll want to create a Brokerage account.

If you're not sure which kind of account to use for your investments, take a look at **Table 14.1** to see Intuit's recommendations.

Table 14.1

Selecting the proper account type for your investment	
INVESTMENT TYPE	ACCOUNT TYPE
Securities for which you want to track a cash balance, such as stocks, bonds, or mutual funds; or a collection of investments in a brokerage account	Investment
A single mutual fund with no cash balance	Single mutual fund
Money market funds	Bank (if you write checks against the fund) or single mutual fund (if you need to track the rate of return)
Certificates of deposit	Bank
Real estate	Asset
IRA accounts, Keogh accounts, variable annuities Unit trusts Real estate investment trusts (REITS) or partnerships	Investment
Treasury bills Fixed annuities, 401(k), 403 (b), pensions Collectibles or precious metals	Investment or asset

Setting Up Your Portfolio

Before you get started setting up your portfolio accounts, you need to decide how much
investment history you want to include in
your records. You can choose from three
options: a complete history, just this year's
information, or what I call the "Aw-the-heck-
with-it" method—just enter your current
investment holdings. (For a detailed rundown of the pros and cons of each method,
see the Quicken User Guide.)

If you choose the complete history option,
you'll need to enter the initial purchase price
for each security and all subsequent transactions. On the plus side, all your reports are
complete, and Quicken can calculate capital
gains accurately. On the minus side, if you
have been investing for several years, that's a
lot of data to enter. However, Intuit recommends this option, and so do I.

If you decide to enter just this year's data,
you'll enter the investment balances as of the
end of last year and then enter all of the transactions for each security since the beginning
of this year. With this method, the information you need to find and enter is more recent
and probably easier for you to obtain. Reports
that deal with events from this year will be
accurate, and if you sell a security, Quicken
will be able to track which lots of it you should
sell to minimize or maximize your short-term
capital gains. This method's disadvantage is
that Quicken will not know the original cost
of the security (called the cost basis), so you
can't get accurate long-term capital gains or
realized gain reports.

Figure 14.1 You can create a new investment account from the Enter a New Investment window.

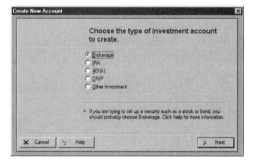

Figure 14.2 Choose the type of investment you are creating.

Figure 14.3 Enter the name of the account, a description, and the name of the financial institution.

If you go with the "Aw-the-heck-with-it" method, you just enter your current investment holdings. This method is the fastest one, and reports that cover events after today will be accurate. On the other hand, you'll have incomplete data for this year and past years, and you won't be able to get reports for capital gains or realized gains.

To create an investment account:

1. Choose Investing > Investing Activities > Create a new investment. The Enter a New Investment window appears (**Figure 14.1**).

2. Decide if you want to set up a new security in an existing investment account or set up an entirely new account (that's what this example does). Click the appropriate radio button, and then click the OK button.

   The Create New Account window appears (**Figure 14.2**).

3. Click the radio button for the type of investment account you want to set up. If you're setting up a single mutual fund, click the Brokerage radio button. Then click Next.

4. In the "About this account" window (**Figure 14.3**), type in the Account Name, an optional description, and the name of the financial institution in which the account is held. Then click Next.

   (continued)

5. In the next setup window (**Figure 14.4**), you are asked if you've applied for online services for this account (for more information about online options, see Chapter 10). If you have, click Yes. Otherwise, click No. Then click Next.

6. The next screen (**Figure 14.5**) asks if the account will allow you to write checks or use a debit card. Click Yes or No, and then click Next.

7. The "What kind of securities" screen appears (**Figure 14.6**). If the investment account will contain multiple investments, click the radio button labeled "Stocks, bonds, or several mutual funds." If this is a single mutual fund account, click the "One mutual fund" radio button. This example assumes that you're creating a multiple investment account (see "To create a single mutual fund investment account" later in this chapter if that's what you want to do). Click Next.

Figure 14.4 If you have applied for online services, click Yes.

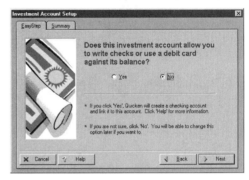

Figure 14.5 Check off the access options your account offers on this screen.

Figure 14.6 This is the screen where you indicate whether this is to be a single mutual fund account or not.

Figure 14.7 Set up the starting point for this account.

Figure 14.8 If this a tax-deferred or tax-exempt account, enter the information here.

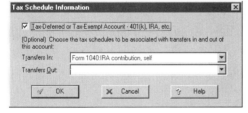

Figure 14.9 The Tax Info button opens a screen that allows you to link the account a tax schedule.

8. The next screen (**Figure 14.7**) establishes the starting point of your account. Enter the starting date and cash balance, and then click Next.

9. Answer Yes or No to whether this account will be tax-deferred or tax-exempt (**Figure 14.8**). If yes, you can click the Tax Info button to link the account to line items on federal tax forms (optional) (see **Figure 14.9**).

(continued)

10. On the Summary screen (**Figure 14.10**), review your entries. If your investment account is linked to a checking account, fill out the Cash Balance section. If you optionally want to add information about the financial institution, click the Info button. The Additional Account Information screen appears (**Figure 14.11**).

11. Click the Done button. The Security Setup screen appears to walk you through adding securities to your investment account.

Figure 14.10 Review your entries and add whatever additional information you need.

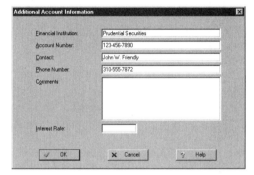

Figure 14.11 Add more information about the financial institution.

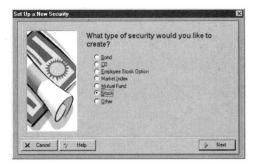

Figure 14.12 Choose the type of security you are adding to your account.

Figure 14.13 Type in the name and the ticker symbol for the security you are adding to your account.

Figure 14.14 You can use the Asset Class and the investment goals to can later sort your investments for analysis.

To add securities to your investment account:

1. If you just created an investment account (the previous topic in this chapter), you're already in the Security Setup screen.

2. If you previously created an investment account and want to add a new security to it, choose Investing > Investing Activities > Create a new investment. Then click the "I want to set up a new security in an existing account" button (refer to **Figure 14.1**). Clicking OK opens the Set Up a New Security screen.

3. Choose the type of security you wish to create and click Next (**Figure 14.12**).

4. Type in a name for the new security, and the ticker symbol (optional) (**Figure 14.13**); then click Next.

5. You can add an Asset Class and your investment goal for this stock on the next screen (**Figure 14.14**).

(continued)

6. In the next screen (**Figure 14.15**), choose the way you want to track the cost basis for this security. Then click Next.

7. The next screen (**Figure 14.16**) sets up how you will track this security. If you choose "Track my holdings," select a start date for the data. Then click Next.

8. On the "Choose an investment account" screen (**Figure 14.17**), specify which of your accounts will contain this investment. Then click Next.

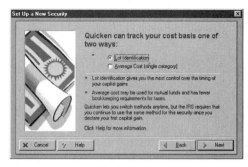

Figure 14.15 The cost basis will determine the amount of tax you'll owe later when you sell the security.

Figure 14.16 Tell Quicken how you want to track the security.

Figure 14.17 This screen lets you choose to which account this investment belongs.

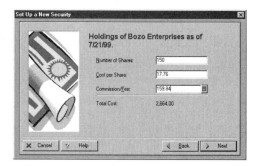

Figure 14.18 Quicken needs to know what your initial outlay was.

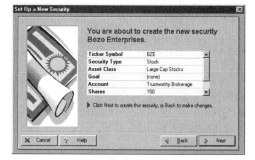

Figure 14.19 On the summary screen, check that all the information is correct.

9. Enter the number of shares you own, the cost per share, and the commission or fee, if any, in the Holdings screen (**Figure 14.18**). Quicken calculates the total cost at the bottom of the window.

10. A final summary screen (**Figure 14.19**) lets you make changes if you made any mistakes. When you're sure everything's OK, click Next. Quicken asks if you'd like to set up another security. Clicking Yes takes you back to the first screen, and clicking No ends the setup process.

SETTING UP YOUR PORTFOLIO

To create a single mutual fund investment account:

1. Follow steps 1 through 7 under "To create an investment account," earlier in this chapter.

2. Answer Yes or No to whether this account will be tax deferred or tax exempt. If Yes, you can click the Tax Info button to link the account to line items for federal tax forms (optional).

3. On the Summary screen, review your entries. Click Done. The Set Up Mutual Find Security screen appears. Add information to this screen, and then click OK. The Create Opening Share Balance screen appears (**Figure 14.20**).

4. Read the instructions on this screen, fill in the blanks if necessary, and then click OK.

   Quicken opens an account register for the new mutual fund account, ready for new entries (**Figure 14.21**).

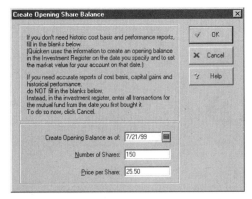

Figure 14.20 Make sure to read the instructions here before you fill in the blanks.

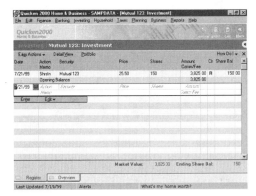

Figure 14.21 Your new mutual fund account now has its own register.

TRACKING AND MANAGING INVESTMENTS

15

After setting up your investment portfolio (see Chapter 14), you need to manage your investments on an ongoing basis. That means updating the share prices of your securities and making entries whenever you buy or sell an investment.

Getting up-to-date quotes on stocks, bonds, and mutual funds is easy if you have an Internet account. If you have a modem and access to the Internet, Quicken can download securities prices and enter them directly into your Portfolio window. Of course, you can always enter information manually if you wish.

Portfolio Maintenance

You use the Portfolio window to get an overview of your investments, and it's an important tool for analyzing how well your investment strategy is working. The Portfolio window has two ways to look at your investments. The Portfolio View (**Figure 15.1**) lets you see all of your investments at once. The Detail View (**Figure 15.2**) zooms in on a particular investment so you can see all the ups and downs of that investment's performance.

Quicken allows you to view and manually enter security prices in either the Portfolio or the Detail View.

To update prices manually in the Portfolio window:

1. Choose Investing > Portfolio View, or press Ctrl U. The Portfolio window appears (refer to **Figure 15.1**).

2. At the top of the Portfolio window, you'll see a date next to "Portfolio as of." If you're updating securities prices for another day (the default is today's date), change this date.

3. Select a security in the Portfolio window by clicking it, and then enter a share price for the displayed date by clicking the appropriate spot in the Mkt Price column, as shown in **Figure 15.3**. You can enter a price as a decimal number or as a fraction. Clicking outside the Mkt Price column saves the new price. Quicken will recalculate the value of that security and your whole portfolio.

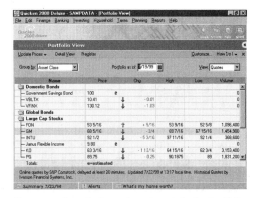

Figure 15.1 See all of your investments in the Portfolio View window.

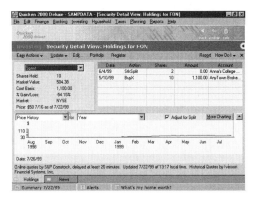

Figure 15.2 The Detail View provides a wealth of information about a security.

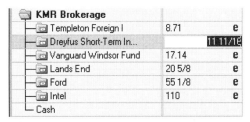

Figure 15.3 In the Portfolio View window, click a price in the Mkt Price column to edit it.

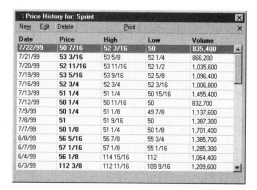

Figure 15.4 The Price History for window shows price quotes you have previously entered or downloaded.

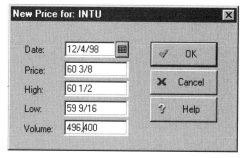

Figure 15.5 The New Price for dialog box only requires that you enter Date and Price, but you can add the High, Low, and Volume information if you wish.

✔ Tips

■ In the Mkt Price column, you can increase or decrease the price by $^1/_{16}$ of a share (0.0625) by pressing the plus (⊞) or hyphen (⊟) key.

■ If the prices in the Portfolio window appear to be incorrect, set the Portfolio View window to today's date, open the Investment register by clicking the Register button at the top of the Portfolio window, then press (Ctrl)(Z) to force a recalculation of your entire portfolio.

To update prices manually in the Security Detail window:

1. In the Portfolio window, double-click on a security name, or click the Detail View button at the top of the window. A security Detail window will appear (refer to **Figure 15.2**).

2. From the Update menu at the top of the window, choose Edit Price History. The Price History window appears (**Figure 15.4**).

3. Make necessary changes to the prices:
   ◆ To enter a new price, click the New button at the top of the window and fill out the New Price for dialog box (**Figure 15.5**); then click the OK button. You're required to fill out only the Date and Price fields; the others are optional.

   ◆ To change a price, click the Edit button, fill out the Edit Price dialog box (which looks almost identical to the New Price dialog box), then click the OK button.

   ◆ To delete a price, select the price that you wish to delete and click the Delete button. Quicken will ask you to confirm the deletion. Click OK to confirm.

To customize the Portfolio View window:

1. From the button bar at the top of the Portfolio View window, click the Customize button to display the Customize Portfolio window (**Figure 15.6**).

2. The View drop-down list at the top of the window contains seven views, or collections of displayed columns, for your portfolio's information. You can customize any of these views. To change between views, choose one from the View drop-down list. To rename a view, click the Change Name button.

3. The scrolling Available Columns list on the left side of the window contains all of the possible choices for the displayed columns in the Portfolio View. To move a column from one column to another, double-click a column name, or select it and use the Add or Remove buttons.

4. To reorder the columns, click a column name in the Displayed Columns list, then use the Move Up or Move Down buttons.

5. You can change the dates shown in Portfolio View by clicking the Date Range button and selecting a time period.

6. When you're done customizing the Portfolio View, click OK.

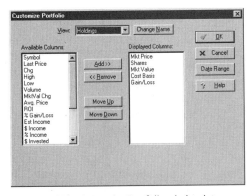

Figure 15.6 The Customize Portfolio window lets you add or subtract columns from the Portfolio View.

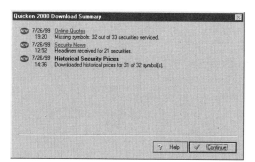

Figure 15.7 After downloading, you get a summary screen letting you know how many online actions successfully concluded.

Getting Online Price Quotes

If you use Online Banking or Bill Payment, you've already set up an Internet connection for Quicken. If you haven't set up the Internet connection, do it now by following the steps under "Setting Up an Internet Connection" in Chapter 10. Quicken uses the same Internet connection information to get investment price quotes as it does to get online banking information.

To download price quotes:

1. Choose Investing > Portfolio View.

2. From the Update Prices menu at the top of the window, choose Get Online Quotes. If you have Quicken Deluxe or Quicken Home & Business, you also have four other options: Get Online Quotes & News; Portfolio Export; Get Asset Classes, which categorizes securities by type; and Get Historical Prices, which downloads the price history for the security going back up to five years. Quicken will connect to the Internet and download the latest prices of your securities.

Quicken then shows you a summary telling you what transpired in the online session (**Figure 15.7**), and enters the prices in your portfolio.

(continued)

✔ Tips

- You can download prices as many times per day you wish, but Quicken stores only one price per day. Every time you download prices, Quicken replaces the prices in your Portfolio with the most recent price.

- The stock symbols in your setup must be exactly the same as those the markets use. If the message "Missing symbols" appears in your Quicken 2000 Download Summary window, check to make sure that your stock symbols are correct.

- Stocks, options, and indexes are updated constantly during the business day, although the quotes you get online are delayed by about 20 minutes. Prices for mutual funds are updated only once per day at 6 p.m. Eastern time.

To customize online quotes:

1. Choose Finance > One Step Update, or click the Online button from the Global bar. The One Step Update Download Selection window appears (**Figure 15.8**).

2. Click Customize.

   The Customize Quicken 2000 Download window opens (**Figure 15.9**). You can also access this window directly as an Action under the Download Summary section of the My Finances home page.

3. In the Quotes & News tab, click the check mark on or off for each security. Choose how far back you want to get security news by selecting a time period from the drop-down list.

4. If you need to find the ticker symbol for a security, click on that security to highlight it in the list, and then click the Look Up Symbol button. Your Web browser will launch, look up the symbol, and display it for you (**Figure 15.10**).

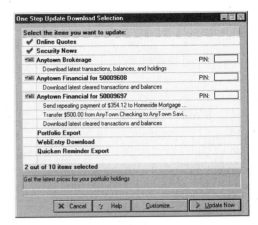

Figure 15.8 Include or exclude stocks from online updating in this window.

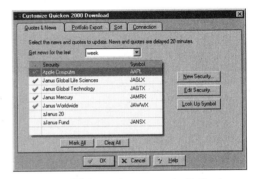

Figure 15.9 Click Customize to open the Customize Quicken 2000 Download window.

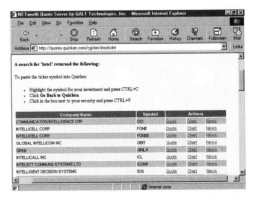

Figure 15.10 Here are the results of looking up a stock symbol on the Web.

Buying and Selling Securities

Most of the transactions in your investment accounts will involve buying or selling securities, but Quicken can handle virtually any sort of investment transaction. **Table 15.1** shows the transactions available in Quicken. Depending on whether you're buying, selling, or moving securities around, the investment process can be quite complex. Refer to the Quicken User Manual to learn about complex investment transactions. I'll limit this example to simple buying or selling.

You can enter investment transactions by using investment forms or by entering information directly into the investment account register. The investment forms are easier to use, especially if you're new to these sorts of transactions. After you become familiar with investment transactions, you may choose to simply enter the information into the investment account register.

Table 15.1

Investment Actions

Action	Description
Buy	Buy security with cash
Capital Gain Long	Receive cash from long-term capital gains distribution
Capital Gain Short	Receive cash from short-term capital gains distribution
Dividend	Receive cash from dividend
Interest Income	Receive cash from interest income
Miscellaneous Expense	Pay miscellaneous expense with cash
Miscellaneous Income	Receive cash from miscellaneous income
Move Shares In	Add shares to account
Move Shares Out	Remove shares from account
Reinvest Dividend	Reinvest in shares of the security with money from dividend or income distribution
Reinvest Interest	Reinvest in shares of the security with money from interest distribution
Reinvest Long	Reinvest in shares of the security with money from long-term capital gains distribution
Reinvest Short	Reinvest in shares of the security with money from short-term capital gains distribution
Return of Capital	Receive cash from return of capital
Sell	Sell security and receive cash
Stock Split	Change number of shares as result of stock split
Transfer Money	Transfer money into or out of this account

To use investment forms for transactions:

1. In the Portfolio View, select the investment for which you wish to enter a transaction.

2. Click the Detail View button at the top of the Portfolio View window.

3. Choose a transaction type from the Easy Actions menu in the button bar (**Figure 15.11**). Depending on which Action you choose, different windows appear. **Figure 15.12** shows the Buy/Add Shares window. Select the investment account to which you want the purchased shares to go, then click Next.

4. You'll need to tell Quicken the source of the funds you'll be using to buy the shares (**Figure 15.13**). Choose a source, then click Next.

Figure 15.11 Begin an investment transaction by clicking the Easy Actions menu in the button bar.

Figure 15.12 The Buy/Add Shares wizard steps you through increasing your security holdings.

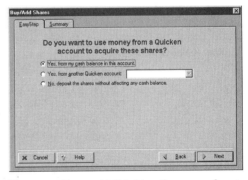

Figure 15.13 You must tell Quicken the source of your investment funds.

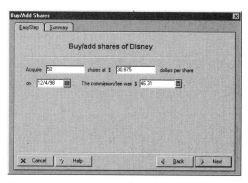

Figure 15.14 Fill out the investment detail window. You can calculate the broker's commission, if any, by clicking the calculator button next to the commission/fee field.

Figure 15.15 Review and approve the investment information in the Summary window to complete your transaction.

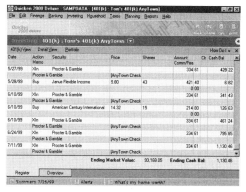

Figure 15.16 The Investment Register lets you see all the transactions in a particular investment account.

5. Fill out the information in the detail window (**Figure 15.14**), then click the Next button.

6. If necessary, make changes in the Summary screen (**Figure 15.15**). Click Done to save your transaction.

To show the Investment Register:

1. From the Portfolio View, select an investment account, then click the Register button at the top of the window. The Register appears (**Figure 15.16**).

2. The Investment Register includes all transactions for all of the securities in the investment account. You can enter the transaction right in the register; for details, see the Quicken onscreen help.

BUYING AND SELLING SECURITIES

GETTING INVESTMENT INFORMATION ONLINE

Good, in-depth information is a key to smart investing. After you have been investing for a while, you'll probably want to take the next step and get more involved in picking mutual funds, stocks, or bonds. That's going to require some research, and you have access to many research tools from within Quicken.

With Quicken's tools, you can research the performance of mutual fund families; check the historical performance of one or more stocks; get investment advice; and receive pointers to other Web sites with excellent investment information.

A good place to start looking for online investment information is at Quicken.com, which you can access from Quicken by choosing Finance > Quicken on the Web > Quicken.com. See Chapter 20 for more about using Quicken.com.

Using Investment Research

Quicken's Investment Research feature makes it easy to get information on stocks and mutual funds. To open the Investment Research window (**Figure 16.1**), choose Investing > Investment Research. The window shows two tabs at the top, called Evaluate and Search.

The Evaluate tab has two panes, Stocks and Mutual Funds. In the Stocks pane, Quicken.com gives you detailed information on one or more stocks for which you enter ticker symbols. The Mutual Funds pane (**Figure 16.2**) offers fund profiles of the specified funds by Morningstar and lets you research performance and holdings of funds you enter.

Switching to the Search tab (**Figure 16.3**), you see a Stocks pane with a Stock Screener, which lets you search for stocks that meet whatever criteria you set, and Popular Searches, a collection of preset searches based on common strategies.

Below that is a pane for Mutual Funds, in which you can get profiles of the Top 25 Funds from Morningstar (the largest mutual fund rating service), a directory of mutual funds by family name, and a Fund Finder that uses custom criteria to find funds that might be of interest.

The third pane is the Bond section, with a search function for research on individual bonds as well as one that ranks the top performing bond mutual funds in 16 categorics.

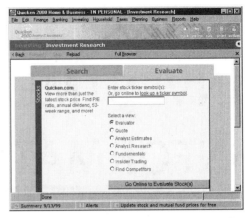

Figure 16.1 Research stocks in the Stocks section of the Investment Research window.

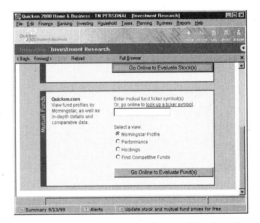

Figure 16.2 You can also research Mutual Funds in the Investment Research window.

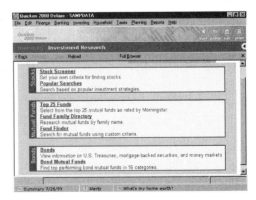

Figure 16.3 The Search tab opens three more avenues for investment research.

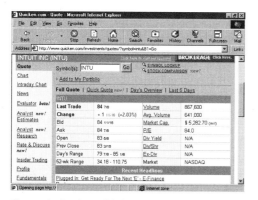

Figure 16.4 Basic stock information is easy to find.

Figure 16.5 Detailed analysis, such as this price chart, is just a click away.

To use Quicken.com to research securities:

1. In the Evaluate pane of the Investment Research window, type a stock ticker symbol in the field under "Enter ticker symbol(s)." Choose the radio button for your area of interest under "Select a view."

2. Click the Go Online to Evaluate Stock button. Quicken connects to the Internet and retrieves information on the stock (**Figure 16.4**).

3. To get other information about the stock, click any of the links on the left side of the screen, such as Chart (**Figure 16.5**), News, Analyst Estimates, or SEC Filings.

✔ Tip

■ You can get information for more than one stock at a time using Quicken.com by entering multiple stock ticker symbols, separated by spaces.

To use Stock Screener and Popular Searches:

1. In the Investment Research window, click the Search tab and then click Stock Screener.

   Quicken connects to the Internet and opens the Stock Search window (**Figure 16.6**). This window contains three kinds of searches that you can use to find stocks, based on whatever criteria you select. You can choose from Popular Searches, EasyStep Search, or Full Search.

2. Choose one of the search types by clicking it, and then follow the onscreen directions. By comparing several stocks against each other, based on the criteria that are of most interest to you, you can make highly informed decisions (**Figure 16.7**).

To use the Morningstar profiles for mutual funds:

◆ In the Investment Research window, enter the ticker symbol for a mutual fund into the Morningstar profiles fields. Then click the appropriate radio button (refer to **Figure 16.2**).

   Quicken connects to the Internet and retrieves the profile you requested (**Figure 16.8**).

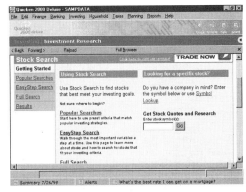

Figure 16.6 The Stock Search window gives you several ways to find stocks.

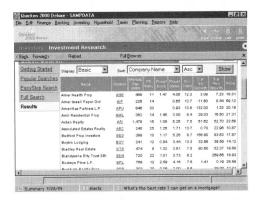

Figure 16.7 Detailed performance lists help you find winners.

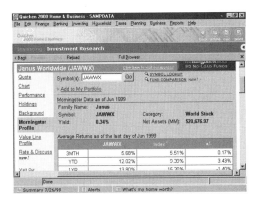

Figure 16.8 Morningstar profiles of mutual funds are valuable tools that make it easier for you to decide on investments.

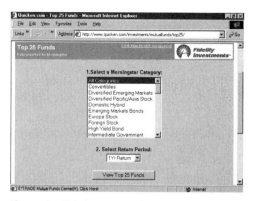

Figure 16.9 Pick the category that matches the kind of mutual fund you're interested in.

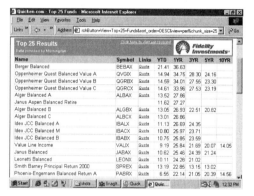

Figure 16.10 The results of your search appear.

To use the Top 25, Fund Family Directory, or Fund Finder:

All three of these features work in much the same fashion, so I'll give an example of how to use just one of them.

1. In the Investment Research window, click the Search tab, and then click Top 25 Funds. Quicken connects to the Internet and displays a criteria selection screen (**Figure 16.9**).

2. From the scrolling list, select a mutual fund category, and then choose the length of return you wish to see from the drop-down list.

3. Click "View Top 25 Funds." Quicken displays the funds ranked by their results over the selected period (**Figure 16.10**).

Getting Investment Information with Quicken.com

Quicken.com has several miscellaneous areas with investment information. The Investments page on the Quicken.com window has three main areas: Tools, Departments, and Investments. To reach this page, choose Finance > Quicken on the Web > Quicken.com, and then click Investments under Departments. Let's look at some of the most interesting features of the Investments page.

◆ Under Departments, IdeaCenter gives you a variety of investment advice from top market mavens, a digest of the best financial news, and a feature about spotting tomorrow's hot investments (**Figure 16.11**).

◆ Again under Departments, NewsCenter provides the latest market and business news, and you can even customize it to highlight news from stocks and mutual funds in your portfolio (**Figure 16.12**).

◆ In the main Investments part of the window, you'll find QuickAnswers, which offers a rotating series of questions about investing, such as "What stocks should I pick?" and "What should I do about my 401(K)?" (**Figure 16.13**).

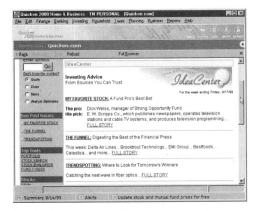

Figure 16.11 IdeaCenter gives you sage investment advice that will stimulate your thoughts and help you make investments decisions.

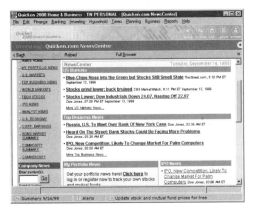

Figure 16.12 You'll find all of the latest business and market news in NewsCenter.

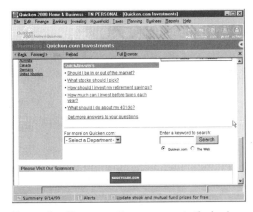

Figure 16.13 If your questions run more to the basics, the QuickAnswers section will provide fast relief.

PART 3

GETTING ANSWERS AND PLANNING FOR THE FUTURE

CREATING REPORTS

I have to admit that before I started using Quicken, my financial house was not exactly in order. Like many people, I had built up a bit too much credit card debt; I balanced my checkbook twice a year, whether it needed it or not; and although I knew that money was coming in and money was going out, I didn't know just where all that money was going.

Quicken's reports, one of its most powerful tools, went a long way toward solving my financial problems by giving me a comprehensive picture of my finances. After using Quicken for just a few months, I had a good record of how much I was spending and where I was spending it. I could also see how much I was spending on interest, which really gave me the impetus to pay off those bills.

One of the best features of Quicken reports is that you can use them to look at your financial data in different ways. You can view your finances in as much or as little detail as you need, and you can pull out just the information that you want. For example, at tax time, I pull a report to show all of my tax-deductible expenditures for the previous year, neatly categorized and totaled. My accountant appreciates it (anything would be better than that shoe box of loose receipts I used to drop on his desk), and because using the reports takes less of his time, it saves me money.

Using Reports

Quicken comes with a variety of report templates that cover most of the questions you may have about your finances. You can customize those reports to zero in on just the information that you want.

Quicken gives you four kinds of reports: EasyAnswer, Standard, Memorized, and QuickReports.

The first three are created in the Reports and Graphs Center (**Figure 17.1**). You can move among different kinds of reports using the tabs at the left side of the Reports and Graph Center window. The first two tabs are the EasyAnswer and Memorized report tabs.

The other four tabs (five in Quicken Home and Business) are labeled with the questions "What do I own and owe?", "How am I spending my money?", "How are my investments doing?", and "What is my tax situation?" If you have Quicken Home and Business, you'll see an additional question: "How is my business doing?" The bulk of your report generation is likely to take place in these tabs.

The main frame displays the report templates for the tab selected. Below the frame, you can specify the dates for the report and choose other parameters that you want the report to contain.

✔ Tip

■ You'll usually view reports on the screen, but you can also print any report. See "Printing Reports" later in this chapter.

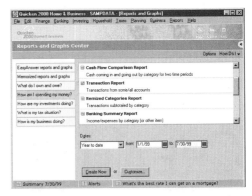

Figure 17.1 The Reports and Graphs Center is your key to squeezing out all your financial information from Quicken's data.

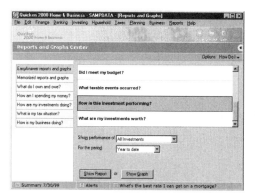

Figure 17.2 EasyAnswer Reports offer quick and basic information about your finances.

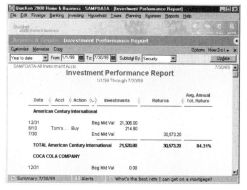

Figure 17.3 An example of a Quicken report, in this case created using the EasyAnswer Reports feature.

Using EasyAnswer Reports

EasyAnswer reports give you quick answers to 10 basic questions, such as "Where did I spend my money?" and "What are my investments worth?" Once you have generated the report, you can customize it at will.

To create an EasyAnswer report:

1. Choose Reports > EasyAnswer Reports. The Reports and Graphs Center window appears with the EasyAnswer tab selected (**Figure 17.2**). This window shows 10 basic questions that you can ask about your finances.

2. Select the question that you want to ask. If necessary, adjust the date range by choosing a new time frame from the drop-down list below the question that you clicked.

3. If you picked a question that requires it, choose a category to narrow your report from the drop-down list below the question.

4. Click the Show Report button, and Quicken displays the report (or graph) on your screen (**Figure 17.3**).

USING EASYANSWER REPORTS

Using Standard Reports

You can use standard reports to get basic information, such as transaction details, net worth, and category transaction reports. They also provide a wide range of investment and tax information.

To create a Standard report:

1. Choose Reports > Reports and Graphs Center. The Reports and Graphs Center window opens.

2. Click one of the tabs to the left of the main frame with a question on it (**Figure 17.4**). The frame displays a number of options for the area you clicked.

3. Select the report that you want to create.

4. If necessary, change the date range of the report by changing the value of the Dates drop-down list of preset ranges, or by typing or selecting dates in the date fields (**Figure 17.5**). Depending on the type of report, there will be one or more fields you can change. Some reports are comparison reports; that is, they compare how you're doing this year with how you did during the same period the previous year.

5. Click the Create button to generate the report (**Figure 17.6**).

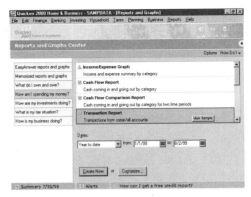

Figure 17.4 Choosing a tab at the left side of the window opens a corresponding set of options to choose from.

Figure 17.5 You can control the date range of your report by using the Dates drop-down list.

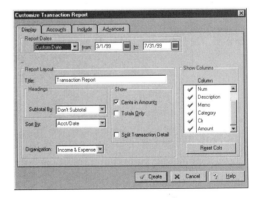

Figure 17.6 Click Create to generate the report.

Customizing Reports

Often the information you get from a Standard Report is *almost* what you need. The good news is that it's easy to customize the report to focus on the information you really want. In many cases, the best way to proceed is to start with a Standard Report and tweak it until it serves your purposes.

You usually customize reports in Quicken with the Customize Report window, although you can make some changes right in the report window.

Creating reports directly from the menu

You can quickly generate reports by clicking Reports on the menu and then dragging down to the area of interest and to the specific report you want (**Figure 17.7**). Quicken will display that report based on the default date range (usually Year to Date—i.e., from January 1 of the current year to today). Once you have created a report, you can modify any of its variables by clicking Customize from the button bar at the top of the page.

You can change the default date range and certain characteristics of the display by selecting Edit > Options > Reports and Graphs or by clicking options in the Reports and Graphs Center window.

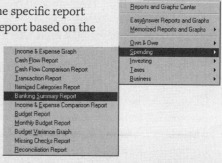

Figure 17.7 You can drag down through the Reports menu to generate reports without going to the Reports and Graphs Center.

To customize reports in the report window:

1. Follow steps 1 through 5 in the previous section, "To create a Standard report."

2. In the Report window, choose one or more of the following formatting options:

   ◆ You can modify the date range of the report by changing the date drop-down lists and then clicking the Update button (**Figure 17.8**).

   ◆ Change the width of the report columns by dragging the column markers to the right or left. When the cursor is over a column marker, the cursor turns into a double-headed arrow, indicating that it is ready for dragging (**Figure 17.9**).

   ◆ You can change other formatting options, such as Sort, Column, or Subtotal, by selecting from the menu at the top of the report (**Figure 17.10**).

3. You can get to the Customize Report window either by clicking the Customize button at the top of an open report or by clicking the Customize button at the bottom of the Reports and Graphs Center screen (refer back to **Figure 17.2**).

   Either way, the Customize Report window opens. The title of the window will change slightly, reflecting the kind of report you're customizing. We will use the Transaction Report as an example.

✔ Tip

■ If you pause the cursor over the title of the report, it turns into a magnifying glass with a C in it. You can then double-click to open the Customize Report window.

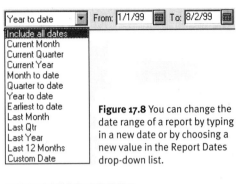

Figure 17.8 You can change the date range of a report by typing in a new date or by choosing a new value in the Report Dates drop-down list.

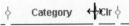

Figure 17.9 You can drag the column markers back and forth to change the column widths.

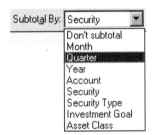

Figure 17.10 The tool bar at the top of the report gives you a simple way to alter the report.

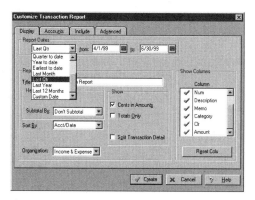

Figure 17.11 Choose the date range from the drop-down list on the Display tab.

To use the Customize Report window:

1. Open the Customize Report window by clicking the Customize button at the top of the open Report window.

   or

   Before you create the report, click Customize instead of Create Now in the Reports and Graphs Center.

2. Choose the date range for the report from the Report Dates drop-down lists in the Customize Transaction Report window's Display tab (**Figure 17.11**).

3. Edit the report title, if desired, by selecting it and typing in a new one.

4. If you want to subtotal your report with a time period, select that period from the Subtotal By drop-down list.

5. Set the sort order using the Sort By drop-down list.

6. Some report types let you choose the organization of the report, either as an Income & Expense report or as a Cash Flow report. Change the drop-down list as you wish.

7. In the Show section, choose to show cents in the amounts of the report, show only the category totals, or show the details of split transactions.

8. In the Show Columns list, you can customize the columns that will be in the report. By default, all columns are on; click the check mark next to a column name to turn off that column. (For example, you might want to turn off the Memo column so that you can see more of the report on your screen without scrolling.)

(continued)

CUSTOMIZING REPORTS

9. Click the Accounts tab (**Figure 17.12**) to open it. If you want to include or exclude certain accounts from your reports, click the check mark next to the account name in the Selected Accounts list. The Account Type, Mark All, and Clear All buttons make it easy to select some or all accounts.

10. Click the Include tab (**Figure 17.13**) to open it. This tab lets you include or exclude particular categories or classes by checking them off in the Select to Include list. You can also match items in your QuickFill lists by choosing items in the Matching section of the window.

11. Click the Advanced tab (**Figure 17.14**) to open it. Here, you can enter an amount and tell Quicken to report on only the transactions that are less than, equal to, or greater than that amount; select what sorts of transactions you want to include; and display transactions based on whether they are cleared or reconciled.

12. When you're done customizing the report, click the Create button.

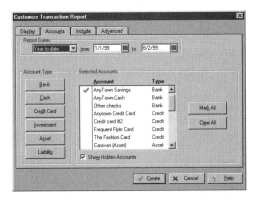

Figure 17.12 The Accounts tab opens another set of parameters you can change to focus your report on your area of interest.

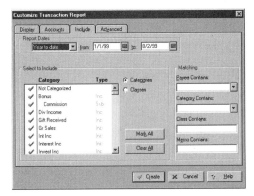

Figure 17.13 The Include tab lets you select among your categories and fine tune your report further using the matching fields.

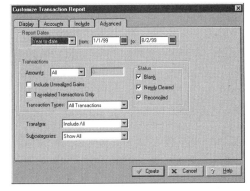

Figure 17.14 The Advanced tab provides another set of controls on the content of your report.

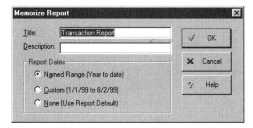

Figure 17.15 Enter the name of a Memorized report in the Memorize Report window.

Using Memorized Reports

Tweaking reports until they are exactly the way that you want them can take a fair amount of effort, and it would be an annoying waste of your time if you had to re-create a custom report every time you needed to see it. When you customize a report, you can save the settings and use them again. These Memorized reports are especially easy to reuse.

To memorize a report:

1. Create a custom report.

2. Click the Memorize button at the top of the report window. The Memorize Report window appears (**Figure 17.15**).

3. Enter a title and a description (optional) for the report. Under Report Dates, choose Named Range, Custom, or None.

4. Click the OK button.

To use a memorized report:

1. Choose Reports > Reports and Graphs Center.

2. Click the Memorized reports and graphs tab and select the report you want to use.

3. Adjust the dates if necessary. Click either Create Now or Customize if you want to change some other parameters.

Or

1. Choose Reports > Memorized Reports and Graphs, and then choose a report you have previously memorized.

2. You can customize your newly created report to your current requirements by modifying the options at the top of the report or by clicking Customize on the button bar.

Using QuickReports

You can create QuickReports directly in the account registers. They can be a list of all the transactions in the register or of a specific set based on a selected transaction.

To create a QuickReport from a specific transaction:

1. Open an account register.

2. Scroll through the register until you find the transaction for which you want a report. Click the transaction to select it.

3. Click the Report menu at the top of the register, and choose either "Amount spent on [category name]" or "Payments made to [payee name]" (**Figure 17.16**). Quicken generates the report (**Figure 17.17**).

To create a QuickReport for the whole register:

1. Open a register.

2. Click the Report button and select Register Report. Quicken generates the report. Like all reports, this one is easily customized and can serve as the starting point for a memorized report as well.

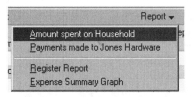

Figure 17.16 QuickReports give you a simple summary of a set of transactions related to the transaction you have selected.

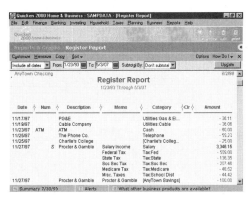

Figure 17.17 A Register Report gives you a customizable record of a single register.

Figure 17.18 The magnifying glass cursor can open a QuickZoom Report and show the details for the selected category.

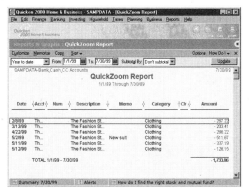

Figure 17.19 This is an example of a QuickZoom Report for the Clothing category.

Figure 17.20 Double-click one of the transactions in a QuickZoom report to see the transaction in the register.

Zooming In on the Details

You can use QuickZoom to examine the information in your reports in greater detail. If you're viewing a report that summarizes the amounts from a category, you can double-click an amount and QuickZoom will take you to another report that shows more detail about the selected item. If you use QuickZoom in a transaction report, Quicken opens the register and shows you the original transaction. QuickZoom lets you "drill down" into your financial information, from the broadest report to the underlying transactions.

To use QuickZoom:

1. Create a report summarizing expenses by category. (You can actually create any sort of report you wish—this is just an example.)

2. In the open report window, move the cursor over one of the amounts in the report until the cursor turns into a magnifying glass with a Z inside (**Figure 17.18**).

3. Double-click the amount of a category.

   A QuickZoom Report opens, showing you the detailed transactions for the category (**Figure 17.19**).

4. To view an original transaction, double-click on an amount in the detailed transaction report window.

   The account register for the transaction will open with the transaction selected (**Figure 17.20**).

Printing Reports

Quicken makes it easy to print reports and lists of all kinds, whether from the Reports section or from other areas of the program, such as account registers or lists.

To print a report:

1. Create a standard or memorized report as described earlier in this chapter.

2. Choose File > Print Report, or press Ctrl P. The Print dialog box appears (**Figure 17.21**).

3. Choose to print to a printer or a file in the Print to section.

4. Under Orientation, choose Portrait (vertical) or Landscape (horizontal) printing.

5. If necessary, use the Page Range section to limit the number of pages you want to print.

6. Checking "Fit to One Page Wide" will scale the width of the report so that it fits on a single page.

7. Click the OK button to print the report.

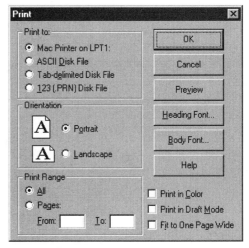

Figure 17.21 The Print dialog box sets up the report for your printer.

Register and List Reports

Register and list reports aren't exactly reports in the same sense as the other types. Quicken allows you to print the current account register or list, but sometimes that's all you need.

To print an account register or a list:

1. Open the account register or list that you want to print.

2. If you're printing a register, choose File > Print Register. If you're printing a list, choose File > Print List. The Print dialog box appears (refer to **Figure 17.21**).

3. Set the print options as required, and click OK.

18

CREATING GRAPHS

When it comes to getting a good overview of your finances, reports are good but graphs are better. Graphs can often illustrate relationships in your finances that numeric reports don't make clear.

Quicken can display your financial data as bar and pie graphs to help you quickly analyze your income and expenses, develop budgets, and determine your net worth.

In addition to their informational benefits, graphs can give you an important emotional boost, as I discovered while working to pay off my consumer debt. I created a bar graph that showed how much debt I owed. Every month, as I made payments, I'd check the graph to see how much the debt bar had shrunk. It felt great to see the downward trend in graphic form as I worked toward my goals—and it felt even better the month that the bar finally hit the zero mark.

As with reports (see Chapter 17 for more about reports), Quicken comes with a variety of templates to get you started using graphs. You can create custom graphs to answer particular questions about your finances.

Using a Standard Graph

Standard graphs provide such information as your net worth, the value of your investment portfolio, and details about your income and expenses. You can customize Standard graphs to suit your own needs. You can create many types of graphs in Quicken, but I'm going to cover only the most commonly used types.

To create a Standard graph:

1. Choose Reports > Reports and Graphs Center to open the Reports and Graphs Center window. Then choose either EasyAnswer reports and graphs or one of the three categories (What do I own and owe, How am I spending my money, or How are my investments doing). Quicken shows the available graphs in the main window (**Figure 18.1**).

2. Select the graph that you want to create.

3. If necessary, change the date range of the graph by changing the value of the Dates drop-down list or by typing in a date or dates in the date fields.

4. Click the Create Now button to generate the graph (**Figure 18.2**).

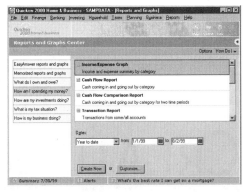

Figure 18.1 You create all of your graphs in Quicken from the Reports and Graphs Center.

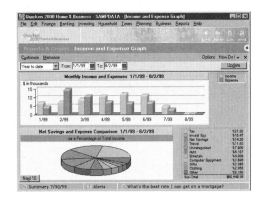

Figure 18.2 This standard Income and Expense graph was created from data entered in the account registers.

USING A STANDARD GRAPH

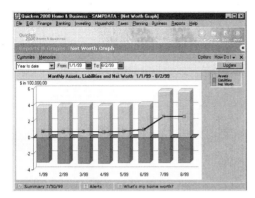

Figure 18.3 A Net Worth graph.

About Net Worth Graphs

Net Worth graphs need a bit of explanation. You calculate your net worth by subtracting your liabilities from your assets. These bar graphs show your assets above the zero line and your liabilities below the zero line, with your net worth appearing as a small red square (hopefully above the zero line!).

To create a net worth graph:

1. Choose Reports > Own & Owe > Net Worth graph. The graph appears for the date range set as the default.

2. If necessary, change the date range of the graph by changing the value of the date range drop-down list or by changing the entries in the date fields.

3. Click the Update button to implement your changes. Quicken generates your Net Worth graph (**Figure 18.3**).

Using QuickZoom to Get More Detail

As with reports, you can use the QuickZoom feature to drill down into your graphs for more detail.

To get more detail with QuickZoom:

1. Create a graph.

2. Move the cursor over one of the colored areas on the graph.

   The cursor will turn into a magnifying glass. After a moment, the dollar value of that segment of the graph will appear (**Figure 18.4**).

3. Double-click a segment of the graph to open another graph showing you more detail (**Figure 18.5**).

4. To get even more detail, double-click a segment of the detailed graph.

   A report window opens, showing you the original transactions that make up the graph segment (**Figure 18.6**).

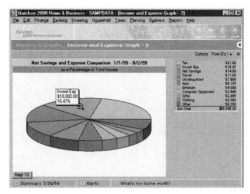

Figure 18.4 Hovering over a region on a graph displays the dollar amount and category for that region.

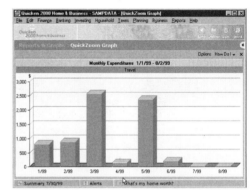

Figure 18.5 Double-clicking shows the detail under the pie graph, presented as a monthly bar graph.

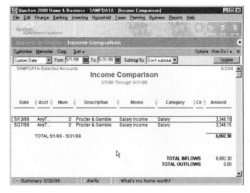

Figure 18.6 Double-click the detailed graph to see a report showing you the original transactions used to create the graph.

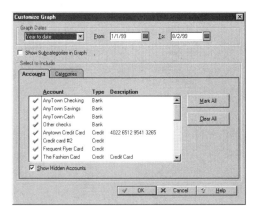

Figure 18.7 You can fine-tune your graphs in the Customize Graph window.

Customizing Graphs

Quicken's standard graph templates are adequate in most cases, but sometimes you'll want to create a custom graph to get specific information. For example, you might want to compare your income with your spouse's, or (if you're really looking for marital trouble) compare your expenses.

To create a custom graph:

1. Create a graph.

2. Click the Customize button at the top of the graph window. The Customize Graph window appears (**Figure 18.7**).

3. If you wish, change the date range of the graph.

4. Click the Accounts tab. Check accounts on or off to narrow the scope of the graph. Repeat as necessary for the Categories and Classes tabs.

5. Click the OK button to create your custom graph.

✔ Tip

- You can also change the display of the graph in the Quicken window. For example, you can choose to view the graphs in a flat, two-dimensional display, rather than the default three-dimensional look.

To change the look of a graph:

1. Create a graph.

2. Choose one or more options from the Options menu at the top of the graph window to open the Options dialog box (**Figure 18.8**).

    ◆ Unchecking Create Report/Graph before Customizing causes the Reports & Graphs Center to open when you choose a graph or report from the menu.

    ◆ Unchecking Show Customize Bar hides the date range drop-down lists and requires you to click the Customize button to make any changes.

    ◆ Draw in 2D creates flat graphs, rather than the attractive 3D default graphs. This is useful if you have a slower PC.

    ◆ Use Patterns Instead of Colors is a good choice if you'll be printing the graph on a monochrome printer. Otherwise, for onscreen displays, the default color display is much clearer.

    ◆ Create All Graphs in Separate Windows (see **Figure 18.3**) gives you bigger versions of multipart graphs in separate, dedicated windows. This is useful if you have a small monitor.

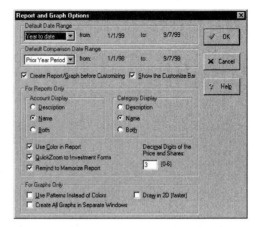

Figure 18.8 Choose one or more graph options from the Options dialog box.

CUSTOMIZING GRAPHS

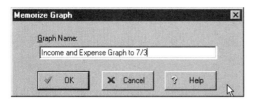

Figure 18.9 After you have customized a graph, you can memorize it and give it a name.

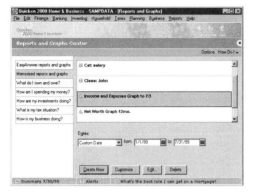

Figure 18.10 Choose a previously memorized report from the Memorized Graphs list.

Using Memorized Graphs

Once you have customized a graph, chances are you're going to want to use it again. Memorized graphs are customized graphs that you have saved for later reuse.

To memorize a graph:

1. Create a custom graph as described previously.

2. Click the Memorize button at the top of the graph window. The Memorize Graph dialog box appears (**Figure 18.9**).

3. Enter a name for the graph.

4. Click the OK button.

To use a memorized graph:

1. Choose Reports > Reports & Graphs Center. Select the Memorized reports and graphs tab and the list appears (**Figure 18.10**).

2. Select a graph (the graphs have a bar graph icon in front of their names) from the list and click the Create Now button at the bottom of the window.

To delete a memorized graph:

1. Choose Reports > Reports & Graphs Center. Select the Memorized reports and graphs tab and the list appears (refer to **Figure 18.10**).

2. Select a graph name from the list and click the Delete button at the bottom of the window.

3. Click the Yes button when Quicken asks you to confirm the deletion.

Printing Graphs

Most of the time, you'll be displaying your graphs onscreen, but on occasion you'll want to print them out to show others. You might want to print an income graph to dazzle a loan officer, for example, or to show friends and relatives what a financial whiz you've become.

To print a graph or chart:

1. Open or create a graph or chart.

2. Choose File > Print Graph.

USING THE PLANNING CENTER

One thing I like about Quicken is that it sheds light on the past, present, and future of my financial life. I can look back to where I've been, deal with my current finances, and create my future financial scenario.

Sometimes I just want to look a little way into the future, so I use the Financial Calendar to see which payments I have scheduled for next month. If my finances were a bit more predictable (that they aren't is a side effect of my life as a freelance writer), I might be interested in creating a yearly budget. However, I do plan to retire someday, so I use Quicken's retirement planners to see whether I'm on track with my savings and investment programs.

The Quicken 2000 family includes several tools that can help you now as well as in the future, including the Debt Reduction Planner, the Retirement Planner, and the Home Purchase Planner. These tools are available in the Deluxe, Home & Business, and Suite versions of Quicken.

In addition, the Planning area includes budgeting and savings goals tools to help you manage your finances in the short term.

In this chapter you'll learn how to use the planners and some of Quicken's other tools that can help you take control of your finances now and plan for your future financial well-being.

Using the Financial Planners

Quicken 2000 (Deluxe version and better) includes several programs that walk you through the process of creating financial plans to meet your specific goals. After asking you a series of questions and drawing on the numbers in your Quicken data file, the programs create a financial action plan for you.

Once all your assumptions are set, you can see what the consequences will be for your future financial status. The Planning Center page (**Figure 19.1**) is arranged around the big budget Life Event Activities you should probably be concerned about—Retirement, College, and Home Purchase, as well as an assortment of other goals.

Each of these areas has its own subset of assumptions and goals and can be investigated in the context of the whole financial picture. Quicken is a very powerful tool for this kind of analysis.

To make your work easier, some of the financial planners include audio and multimedia movies that show examples and illustrate financial concepts. To hear the sounds and view the movies, you must have the Quicken 2000 CD in your CD-ROM drive. You can also run the planners without the CD (but you'll miss the multimedia treats).

Figure 19.1 The Planning Center includes a good selection of Life Event Planners.

Quicken's main planners

Here's a rundown of Quicken's main planners.

- The Quicken Retirement Planner program probes your savings and investment plans and tells you whether your current plan (if you have one) is adequate to meet your needs when you retire. If it's not adequate, the planner will come up with a new plan to help you meet your goals.

- College Plans is a wizard that will help you determine how to get ready for the cost of college for your children. It will estimate the costs, based on current trends, and allow you to set up a plan to pay for it all.

- The Home Purchase Planner is designed to help you answer the question "Can I afford that house?" It also offers some guidance on the decision of whether to buy or rent.

- Many people are carrying too large a load of consumer debt, and the Debt Reduction Planner will show you how to get out of debt faster and save money while doing it. If you follow the recommendations in this planner, you can save hundreds or even thousands of dollars in interest payments.

(continued)

- You can use the Save More Planner to establish some realistic expectations for how much you should be able to put away as savings. It sorts through your income and your expenses. Links to other areas of the Quicken program will help you improve your financial situation.

- Special Purchase Plans is another segment of the Planning Center that will help you develop a strategy for meeting future costs. You specify what it is, how much it will cost, and how you'll pay for it, and Quicken will help you make sure that when the time comes to spend, you'll be financially ready.

- The "What-If" Event Scenarios were developed in conjunction with the Institute of Certified Financial Planners. They allow you to go back to your original assumptions, modify them, and see what the impact on your overall plan might be. Quicken compares the current plan with the optional plan to help you make an informed decision.

Because you'll use each planner in a similar way, I'll go into only two in detail here: the Retirement Planner and the Debt Reduction Planner.

Figure 19.2 The Retirement Planner is the center of the financial planning module.

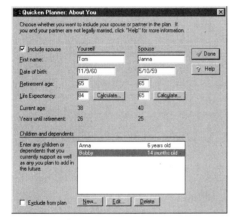

Figure 19.3 Begin the setup process by telling Quicken about yourself.

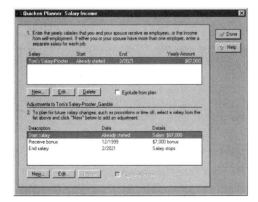

Figure 19.4 The Salary Income screen lists the salaries and adjustments of the plan's participants as well as adjustments to them.

The Retirement Planner

The Retirement Planner is the centerpiece of the entire Quicken Planning scheme. Entering the data takes about half an hour, but once you've done it, you have the basis for making a whole range of decisions about your financial future. Some information is taken from data already in your accounts, but you can modify any assumption to tailor the program to your needs. The database you build as you set up the Retirement Planner is also used by other parts of the Quicken planning system as you evaluate your options on a number of issues.

To set up the Retirement Planner:

1. Choose Planning > Retirement Planner. The Introduction screen (**Figure 19.2**) opens with the question "Can I retire when I want to?" Read the introductory information, and then click Next to move on.

2. In the About You screen, click the underlined hypertext "here" to open the About You dialog box (**Figure 19.3**) and give Quicken the information it needs.

3. Fill in your (and your spouse's, if you have one) personal information and then click Done. Click Next. The Salary page opens.

4. Click on the underlined hypertext "here" in the Salary box to open the Quicken Planner: Salary Income screen (**Figure 19.4**).

(continued)

5. Click New to open the Add Salary dialog box (**Figure 19.5**). Type in the appropriate information and use the pull-down menus to enter the appropriate dates. Then click OK to return to the Salary Income screen.

6. Now click the New button under the Adjustments area at the bottom of the screen. Then, in the Add Salary Adjustment box, enter information about job changes, promotions, and other events that will have an impact on your earnings. Click OK to return to the Salary Income screen.

7. Repeat steps 5 and 6 for all sources of salary income. Then click Done. This returns you to the Salary summary page. Click Next to go to the Retirement Benefits section.

8. Click on the underlined hypertext "here" in the Retirement Benefits box to open the Retirement Benefits screen (**Figure 19.6**).

9. Click the Estimate button to open the calculation worksheet (**Figure 19.7**) for yourself (and your spouse) to see a rough estimate of your annual social security benefits. Enter the data required, and then click OK.

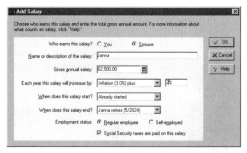

Figure 19.5 Fill in the Add Salary form for each salary.

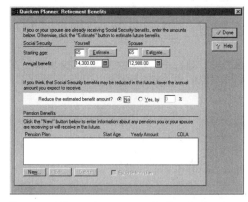

Figure 19.6 The Retirement Benefits form is the place to enter Social Security and other pension benefits.

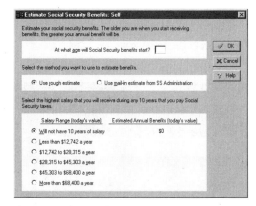

Figure 19.7 The Social Security Benefits calculator makes an estimate of your income from that source.

THE RETIREMENT PLANNER

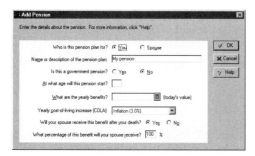

Figure 19.8 Enter private pension income in the Add Pension screen.

Financial Planner Limitations

Although Quicken's financial planning tools give you valuable information and viable action plans, you shouldn't rely on them as your sole source for financial planning.

The world of finance is constantly changing and the subtleties of economic life defy the broad-brush approach of even the most sophisticated electronic advisor. Ultimately, economic decisions are deeply personal, and an understanding of your individual needs is key to making the right decisions.

Electronic financial planners are a good guide, but don't take them as gospel. And before you make any big financial moves, it's always a good idea to consult your accountant and/or a financial planner.

Quicken recognizes its own limitations and provides, as the last but not least important item on the Planning menu, a section that you access by choosing Planning > Professional Planning Resources. There you will find information about professional planners and the Institute of Certified Financial Planners.

10. Click New at the bottom of the Retirement Benefits screen to enter any other pension benefits that will be part of your retirement income. The Add Pension form (**Figure 19.8**) opens so you can enter the appropriate information. When you're done, click OK.

11. Click Done to return to the Retirement Benefits page. Click Next to move to the next section, Other Income.

12. Click the underlined hypertext "here" in the Other Income box and, in the form that appears, enter other forms of income (gifts, inheritance, royalties, etc.) but not Savings and Investments or Income from assets such as rental property. If you have no other income, click Next to go to the Taxes and Inflation section.

13. Continue to fill in the information in the same manner through the remaining sections: Savings & Investments, Homes & Assets, Loans & Debt, and Expenses. In the end, you will have created the complex model Quicken uses to predict your economic future.

✔ Tips

■ You can review your plan by choosing Planning > Planning Center, which shows you the plan results as well as all the other goals you have set (refer to **Figure 19.1**).

■ From the Planning Center, you can change underlying assumptions, try out alternative plans, work out a program of debt reduction, and access the other planning functions Quicken offers.

THE RETIREMENT PLANNER

Reducing Consumer Debt

Paying off your credit card and loan debts is an important step toward financial happiness. If you don't pay off your credit card and loan bills in full every month, the bank charges you interest to compensate for your use of its money. Unfortunately, interest payments aren't a good deal for you; you could spend the money that you pay in interest in far more productive ways.

Quicken's Debt Reduction Planner uses a simple philosophy. It analyzes your debt and helps you pay off the cards with the highest interest rate first, which lets you get out of debt faster while paying less interest.

Spending Savings to Reduce Debt

If you already have some money saved, you might question the wisdom of taking money out of your savings or investment accounts to help pay off your consumer debt. Although it is a smart idea to have a financial cushion, you need to ask yourself if your money is working for you in the best way.

For example, assume that you have $2,000 in an investment that is earning 10 percent interest, but your credit cards are charging you 16 percent interest. At the end of the year, you'll have lost money by not paying off your credit cards. You're better off reducing your debt as quickly as possible.

Figure 19.9 The Welcome screen for the Debt Reduction Planner tells you to insert the CD-ROM so you can see its informational movies.

Figure 19.10 The first movie about Debt Reduction explains why the Planner is an important tool.

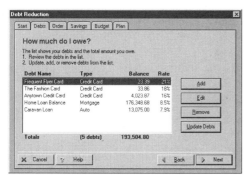

Figure 19.11 The How much do I owe? screen is the starting point for the process of setting up a debt reduction plan.

To use the Debt Reduction Planner:

1. Choose Planning > Debt Reduction Planner. The Start screen of the planner appears (**Figure 19.9**). Click Next.

   If the Quicken 2000 CD is in your machine's CD-ROM drive, Quicken will play a brief movie explaining the purpose and methods the Debt Reduction Planner uses (**Figure 19.10**). Without the CD, you'll go straight to work.

2. After you've viewed the movies (or not), click the Next button to open the Debts screen.

   The planner consults your Quicken data file, gathers all of your debt information, and displays it in a scrolling list (**Figure 19.11**). Initially, it includes all of the debts in your Quicken file; click a debt and click the Remove button to remove the debt if it has a zero balance or if you don't want to include it in the debt reduction plan. Then click Next.

   (continued)

3. In the Edit Debt Reduction screen (**Figure 19.12**), you'll give the planner detailed information about each debt. The planner already knows the balance owed. In the Type of loan pop-up menu, choose Auto, Credit Card, Home Equity, Mortgage, Personal, or Other.

4. Enter the average monthly payment that you actually make, if it's different from the minimum payment. You don't need to be too picky about this figure; just get it in the ballpark.

5. Enter the minimum monthly payment.

6. Enter the annual interest rate for the loan or credit card. Click OK.

7. Repeat steps 4 through 7 for each of your debts that has a balance remaining. Naturally, if a credit card has a zero balance, you don't need to worry about including it in a repayment plan. When you get through all of the Edit Debt Reduction screens, click Next.

8. The planner calculates your debt situation and displays the "How am I doing now?" screen (**Figure 19.13**). This screen tells you when you can expect to pay off your debts if you make no changes to your payment. Click Next to move to the next section, where you'll begin formulating your action plan to get out of debt sooner.

9. The Order section begins with a screen that outlines the steps you'll take next. Read this information, and then click Next.

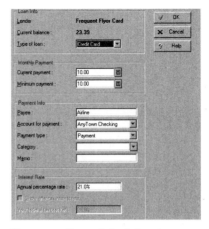

Figure 19.12 The next step is to enter more detailed information about each of your debts.

Figure 19.13 The How am I doing now? screen is a snapshot of your current situation.

REDUCING CONSUMER DEBT

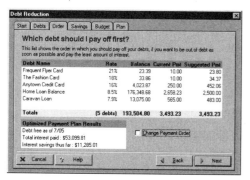

Figure 19.14 The Which debt should I pay off first? screen presents an initial strategy for debt repayment and shows its results in the box at the bottom.

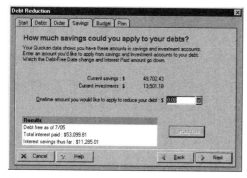

Figure 19.15 You are encouraged to apply some of your savings to reducing your debts.

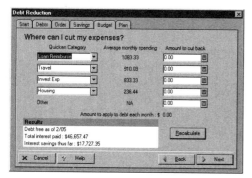

Figure 19.16 You may be able to cut back on some of your expenses and apply that money to debt reduction.

10. The "Which debt should I pay off first?" screen (**Figure 19.14**) shows you the planner's suggested order of paying off your debts, based on the interest rate for each debt, with higher rates listed first. If you want to reorder the debts for some reason (for example, because you prefer to pay off one debt before another), you can click the Change Payment Order checkbox. This isn't recommended, because Quicken has already put the list into its most cost-effective order. After the debts are in order, click Next.

11. The planner plays a movie explaining why it's a good idea to tap your savings to reduce debt now. Click Next; Quicken then taps into your Quicken data file once again to check the values of your bank, cash, and investment accounts (**Figure 19.15**). You should enter an amount you're willing to pay to reduce your debt immediately. (See the "Spending Savings to Reduce Debt" side-bar for more information.) Note the savings shown at the bottom of the screen. Click Next.

12. If you can squeeze just a bit out of your monthly budget and throw that money at bills, money will often come back to you in the form of savings on interest payments. Quicken shows another movie on tracking expenses. Click Next.

13. In the "Where can I cut my expenses?" screen (**Figure 19.16**), Quicken shows you some of your most common extra expenses. Enter how much more you're willing to pay toward your debt each month. Click Next.

(continued)

REDUCING CONSUMER DEBT

14. In the Plan section (yes, you're almost done), you can review your Action Plan and print it out for later reference (**Figure 19.17**). Click Next, and then click Done to exit the Debt Reduction Planner.

15. The Debt Reduction screen (**Figure 19.18**) tells you the results of your plan, including how much you'll save in interest and how much sooner you'll pay off your debt. A handy graph shows you the results of your saner approach to debt. If you want to see the effects of using more savings or paying even more per month, enter that information here and then click Recalculate.

16. Click Payment Schedule to see a detailed breakdown of how much you'll be paying and when (**Figure 19.19**).

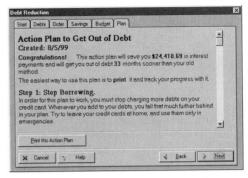

Figure 19.17 The Scenario offers suggestions for increasing your savings.

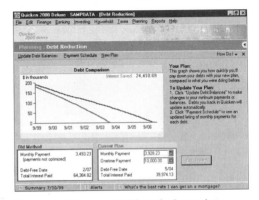

Figure 19.18 The results in the Debt Comparison graph should convince you of the importance of adhering to the plan.

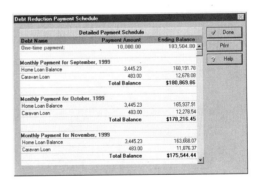

Figure 19.19 The Payment Schedule shows how much you will pay each creditor every month and the balances remaining.

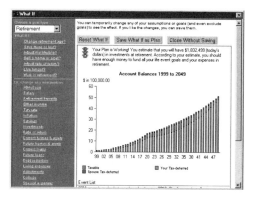

Figure 19.20 The What If page opens with a graph of your existing plan.

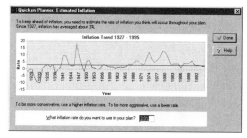

Figure 19.21 The Estimated Inflation window shows the historical rate and allows you to set the projected rate for your plan.

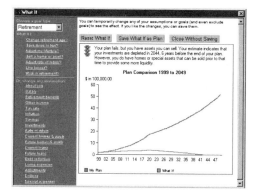

Figure 19.22 The Plan Comparison graph shows that the adjustment you have made results in the failure of your plan.

Using "What-If" Event Scenarios

The "What-If" Event Scenario feature of Quicken's Planning Center is designed to let you try out a number of options and see what works best for your own personal needs. You can trade off short-term pleasure for long-term wealth or choose to live high on the hog today and live in reduced circumstances in your old age.

You can also change your presuppositions about what the economy will do in the future and see what the result will be.

To set up alternative scenarios:

1. Choose Planning > "What-If" Event Scenarios.

   The What If screen (**Figure 19.20**) opens with a graph of your projected account balances for each year covered by your plan and a sidebar with the variables you can experiment with.

2. Choose the goal type from the drop-down menu at the top of the sidebar. Then select either a scenario from the "What if I" section just below the goal or, to change one of the underlying assumptions, choose it from the box below that and click on it. For example, we'll choose to change the rate of inflation and click on "Inflation."

3. The Estimated Inflation screen (**Figure 19.21**) opens. In this example, we'll adjust the rate of inflation to a less optimistic figure of 7%. Type this amount into the inflation rate box at the bottom of the screen, and then click Done.

   Quicken returns to the What If page (**Figure 19.22**). Note that the plan now fails.

(continued)

4. To make a correction, pick another variable from the sidebar (a What If or an assumption). Let's try increasing the Rate of return on our investments to stay ahead of the inflation rate. Click "Rate of return" from the assumption list.

5. In the Return screen (**Figure 19.23**), let's try bringing the rate up to 12%. Type this amount in the box at the bottom of the screen, and then click Done.

The What If window opens again (**Figure 19.24**) and now your plan is again liquid, though not as flush as it was in its original form. You can continue these manipulations as long as you want, and, if you wish, you can replace the previous plan by clicking Save What If as Plan at the top of the screen.

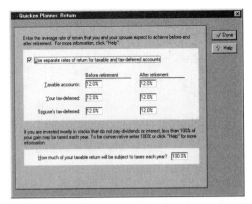

Figure 19.23 Adjusting the rate of return on your investments will obviously have an impact on the plan.

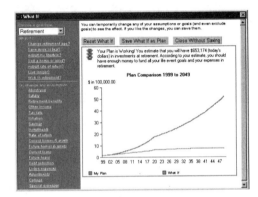

Figure 19.24 The second revision of the plan has brought it back to life, even if it is not as optimistic as the original assumptions had made it.

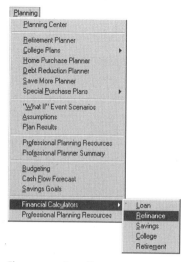

Figure 19.25 From the menu, you can choose the Loan, Refinance, Savings, College, or Retirement calculator.

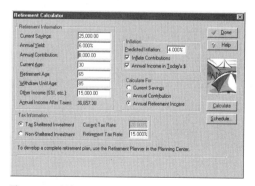

Figure 19.26 The Retirement Calculator.

Age	Deposit	Income	Balance
34	9,358.87	0.00	82,084.71
35	9,733.22	0.00	96,743.02
36	10,122.55	0.00	112,670.15
37	10,527.45	0.00	129,957.81
38	10,948.55	0.00	148,703.83
39	11,386.49	0.00	169,012.56
40	11,841.95	0.00	190,995.26
41	12,315.63	0.00	214,770.61
42	12,808.26	0.00	240,465.11
43	13,320.59	0.00	268,213.60
44	13,853.41	0.00	298,159.83

Figure 19.27 When we adjust our contributions for inflation, they appear in the schedule.

Using the Financial Calculators

Quicken (both the Basic and Deluxe versions) includes five financial planning calculators to help you get quick answers when you're considering a financial move, such as taking on a new mortgage. The financial planning calculators all work in basically the same way—except that the information you enter and the calculations Quicken makes vary. Most of the calculators work in the same way. In this example, let's use the Retirement Calculator.

To use a financial calculator:

1. Choose Planning > Financial Calculators, and then choose the type of calculator that you want from the five shown in the menu (**Figure 19.25**). We will use the Retirement Calculator as an example.

2. In the calculator screen that opens (**Figure 19.26**), enter the appropriate information and click Calculate. Quicken displays the results. In this example, you may choose Current Savings, Annual Contribution, or Annual Retirement Income.

3. Click Schedule to display the amount of each year's contribution with the amounts adjusted for inflation, if you have selected that option (**Figure 19.27**).

Using
Quicken.com

Quicken is a terrific tool for helping you manage your money. To make smart financial decisions, you're going to need up-to-date financial and investment information. That's where Quicken.com, Intuit's huge Web site at www.quicken.com, comes in.

Quicken.com offers up-to-the-minute news, price quotes, and information about the securities markets; tips from financial experts; access to online stock brokerages; retirement planning tools; and current tax information, including explanations of wacky changes Congress makes in the tax code.

Intuit used to include some of this information, such as a Mutual Fund Finder program, on the Quicken CD-ROM. But the information quickly became out of date and useless, so Intuit removed the Mutual Fund Finder from the CD-ROM and moved the information onto the Web, where Intuit can update it frequently.

The Web site tries to cover every aspect of your financial life by organizing its content into 10 departments: Investments, Home & Mortgage, Insurance, Banking & Credit, Small Business, Retirement, Life Events, Taxes, Saving & Spending, and Financial Forums. Alas, I barely have room to scratch the surface. But do spend some time browsing the site; it will be time well spent.

Getting Around on Quicken.com

Before you start browsing the site, you should know what equipment and software you need to view Quicken.com. At a minimum, you'll need the following:

◆ A modem or other connection device. If you're using a modem (most people are), its speed should be at least 28.8 kilobits per second (Kbps). Most modems currently sold are 33.6 or 56 Kbps. If you're lucky enough to have a faster connection to the Internet, such as a cable modem, a DSL or ISDN line, or a local area network, so much the better.

◆ An account with an Internet Service Provider (ISP). An ISP sells access to the Internet. When you sign up with an ISP, you usually get an e-mail account and the ability to create your own Web site, as well as access to the various Internet services.

◆ You won't need separate Web browsing software, because Quicken can call on the copy of Microsoft Internet Explorer already installed under Windows 95 or 98. Quicken can display Web information in its own windows, or you can use the regular Internet Explorer browser window.

The process of getting an account with an ISP and signing onto the Internet is beyond the scope of this book, so I will assume you've taken care of that part.

To get started with Quicken.com, choose Finance > Quicken on the Web > Quicken.com. You should see a screen like the one shown in **Figure 20.1**. If you get to Quicken.com and the screen looks utterly different, chances are Intuit has redesigned the site since I wrote this book in the summer of 1999. Don't panic; companies are forever changing their Web sites. Just poke around until you find what you're looking for.

Figure 20.1 When you log on to Quicken.com, this page shows you the way to the site's helpful information.

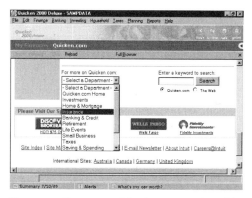

Figure 20.2 Choose one of the departments from this pop-up menu to find specific information.

Along the left side of the screen, in the Departments navigation bar, you'll see Quicken.com's department names. Click a name to open that department's page. Financial news takes up the middle of the window, and a Mini Portfolio table appears on the right.

At the bottom of the browser window (not shown in **Figure 20.1**) is a navigation pop-up menu (**Figure 20.2**) that reveals the Quicken.com department names. Choose one of the departments from the pop-up menu to tell your browser to go there. These are the same departments that appear in the navigation bar on the left side of the screen; the difference is that the navigation pop-up menu is available anywhere on the Quicken.com site, whereas the left navigation bar changes depending on which department you're in.

✔ Tips

- If you need to return to a previous page, click the Back button at the top of the Quicken browser window.

- You can click the Quicken.com logo at the top of most pages on the site to return to the Quicken.com home page.

- If you would rather use the Internet Explorer browser window, click the "Full Browser" button at the top of the Quicken browser window. The page you're currently viewing will open in an Internet Explorer window. Use the Windows Task Bar to get back to Quicken. In many of the examples in this chapter, I've chosen to use pictures from Internet Explorer rather than Quicken's built-in browser, because the Internet Explorer screens are a bit larger and easier to read in the small size the book page permits. But you should use whatever browser you're most comfortable with.

Finding Investment Information

The Quicken.com department used most often is Investments. It's impossible to discuss everything you could do in the Investments department in the amount of space that I have here, so I'll focus on just a few common tasks.

To find a security quote:

1. If you're interested in a quote on a particular security, and you know the security's ticker symbol, type the symbol in the Quotes and Research box next to "Enter symbol." Click the Go button and a detailed quote page for the security appears (**Figure 20.3**).

2. If you're interested in any other information about the same security, choose it from the links down the left side of the page, under the security's name. For example, after you click the Chart link, you'll see a page like **Figure 20.4**

3. Continue your research on the stock by clicking other links from the left column or modifying the type of chart or the period it covers with the menus above it.

   You can add other stocks to the chart by typing their symbols into the box at the top. Quicken will even help you find the stock's competitors with the Stock Comparison lookup feature next to the box.

✔ Tip

- For more information on getting stock information using Quicken.com, see Chapter 16, *Getting Investment Information Online*.

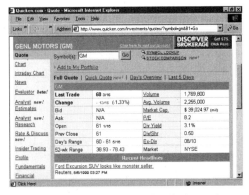

Figure 20.3 Type a stock's symbol in the box under "Quotes and Research" and click the Go button to see information about a particular security.

Figure 20.4 Click the Chart link on the quotes page to see a chart like this one.

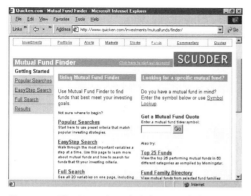

Figure 20.5 The Mutual Fund Finder page helps you find information about mutual funds.

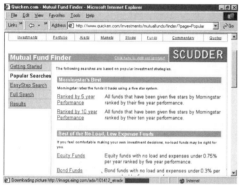

Figure 20.6 The Mutual Fund Finder page has several standard searches to make finding mutual funds easier.

Figure 20.7 This window shows the results of a mutual fund search.

Choosing a Mutual Fund

Thousands of mutual funds are available, and each fund has its own investment objectives. Selecting a mutual fund that meets your criteria for investment is fairly easy using Quicken.com, because it contains detailed information on almost all funds.

To find a mutual fund:

1. From the Quicken.com home page (shown in **Figure 20.1**), click "Pick Top Funds" from the "Top Features" section at the upper left. The Mutual Fund Finder page appears (**Figure 20.5**).

2. Click the "Popular Searches" link. A list of canned (but still useful) searches appears (**Figure 20.6**).

3. Click a search that interests you—for example, "Ranked by 5 year Performance." The Mutual Fund Finder will show the results of your search (**Figure 20.7**).

4. You can refine your search by changing the variables listed above the chart as Display and Sort, or by using the EasyStep wizard to go step by step through a more customized process. If need be, you can go to a more sophisticated Full Search.

(continued)

✔ Tips:

- You can find more information on mutual funds on the Mutual Funds page (**Figure 20.8**), that you can access by clicking "Funds" on the navigation bar near the top of most screens.

- For more information on getting mutual fund information using Quicken.com, see Chapter 16, *Getting Investment Information Online.*

Figure 20.8 The Mutual Funds page has additional information and tools to help you choose a fund that's right for you.

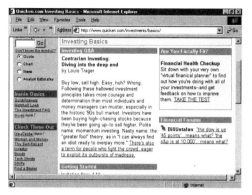

Figure 20.9 Use the navigation bar on the main Investing Basics page to get quick answers to your questions.

Figure 20.10 Find the question that you want answered in the QuickAnswers list.

Insights on Investing

Investing can be confusing. The terminology is often complex and arcane, with weird acronyms and convoluted explanations. Do you know what an index fund is? Why is Morningstar important? What does it mean to sell a stock short? Are DRIPs good for you? Thankfully, Quicken.com has a place you can go to get answers to these questions.

To get answers to basic questions about investing:

1. In the main Investments page, scroll down and click Basics. The main Investing Basics page appears (**Figure 20.9**).

2. In the navigation bar on the left side of the page, click QuickAnswers. The QuickAnswers page appears (**Figure 20.10**).

3. Find the question that you want answered in the QuickAnswers list, and then click the question to jump to its answer page. If you can't find the question that you want answered in the list, look through the Related Links navigation bar on the left side of the page for a section of the site that might help you.

Getting Tax Information

The more information you have about taxes, the more likely you are to make intelligent decisions when tax time comes. The Taxes section of Quicken.com has a lot of general tax information and a tax estimating tool—and you can even download federal and state tax forms from the site.

To find tax tips and advice:

1. From the main Quicken.com page, scroll down and click Taxes. The main Taxes page appears (**Figure 20.11**).

2. Under the heading on the right side of the page entitled "Tax Topics," find the category of information that you need, and then click it to jump to an information page.

Figure 20.11 Find the category of information that you need from the main Taxes page.

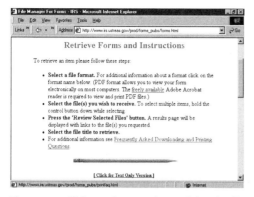

Figure 20.12 Click a tax form to select and download it from the government's Web server.

Downloading tax forms

Quicken.com lets you download federal and state tax forms from the Internal Revenue Service and state revenue office Web sites. You can then print these forms and use them to file your taxes. The files are in a variety of formats, depending on the sites they come from, but Adobe Acrobat format (sometimes called PDF files, for Portable Document Format) is the best one for Windows users. To read Acrobat files, you need to install the free Acrobat Reader program. It comes on the Quicken Deluxe 2000 CD-ROM, it's available on the Quicken.com Web site, or you can download it from Adobe's Web site at http://www.adobe.com.

To download tax forms:

1. In the navigation bar on the left side of the main Taxes page, click the link "Federal Forms." The Forms page appears (**Figure 20.12**).

2. Scroll down the list until you find the tax form or forms that you want to download. Click the title of a form to select it; if you want multiple forms, hold down the (Ctrl) key while selecting.

3. Click the "Review Selected Files" button. On the resulting File Request Results page, click on the name of each selected file to download it to your hard disk.

GETTING TAX INFORMATION

Finding Low-Rate Credit Cards

Credit cards are handy to use, but they can be a major source of financial frivolity. If you don't pay off your credit card balance in full every month, you rack up interest charges. If you can't avoid carrying a balance, you can at least try to minimize the amount of interest you're paying by finding a credit card with a low interest rate.

Quicken.com's Banking & Borrowing area has a list of the credit card providers with the lowest rates as well as other useful information, such as mortgage interest rates, savings account interest yields, and general banking information.

To find low-rate credit cards:

1. From the main Quicken.com page, choose "Banking & Credit" from the navigation bar on the left. The main Banking & Credit page appears (**Figure 20.13**).

2. In the navigation bar on the left, click "Credit Cards." The Credit Card page appears (**Figure 20.14**).

Figure 20.13 In the navigation bar on the left side of this page, click "Credit Cards."

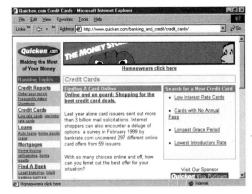

Figure 20.14 Indicate your requirements, and then click Go to start the search for the best credit card and bank rates.

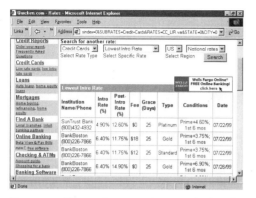

Figure 20.15 The results screen shows a selection of credit cards, ranked according to your criteria.

Figure 20.16 You can find other interest rate information by choosing from the pull-down menus in this box.

3. Choose a primary search criterion from the "Search for a New Credit Card" box and click on it. For example, if a low interest rate is the most important criteria about a credit card for you, click "Low Interest Rate Cards." If you're looking to consolidate higher-rate cards, you might prefer to pick "Lowest Introductory Rate."

   The results screen appears (**Figure 20.15**) ranked by the parameter you chose.

   From here, you can change the search using the pull downs above the list. You can even make quick searches for other interest rates, choosing from the options in the pull-down windows that appear for the rate type you have selected. **Figure 20.16** shows how you can get rates for four-year automobile loans in Birmingham, Alabama.

FINDING LOW-RATE CREDIT CARDS

Other Areas of Interest at Quicken.com

Each of the 10 departments on the Quicken.com site has its own wealth of information. (It also has, as you have probably noticed, quite a bit of advertising.) The Life Events department (**Figure 20.17**) focuses on some of the big-ticket items in many of our lives—College, Weddings, Parenting, Travel, and Retirement.

The Saving and Spending department (**Figure 20.18**) is sort a catch-all for good economic advice.

The Financial Forums area (**Figure 20.19**) is a collection of wide-ranging forums on stocks, insurance, and other issues. Here you can read what other people have to say and add comments of your own.

In general, you will find that Quicken.com and all the links it provides are about as rich a resource for economic advice and research as you are likely to find without paying for it.

Figure 20.17 The Life Events screen helps you plan for life's big expenditures.

Figure 20.18 The Saving and Spending department tells you lots of things you probably should already know.

Figure 20.19 The Financial Forums offer space for a free-flowing exchange of information, misinformation, and gossip that you can sort through.

USING QUICKEN FAMILY LAWYER

21

To deal effectively with all aspects of your financial life, you're going to need to prepare a number of legal documents. For example, every adult (and especially anyone who is a parent) should have a will in the event of his or her death. Similarly, you might want to specify in advance health care instructions in case of severe accidents, or arrange for organ donations.

There are plenty of other legal documents that you might want to cover as well. You might need to create a bill of sale for an automobile. When we send our son across the country to visit his grandparents, we give him a letter with authorization for medical treatment and insurance information, just in case. Or you might own rental property and need applications for prospective renters.

At one time, you had to pay for an attorney to prepare such documents. But these documents are mostly standard, and that's where Quicken Family Lawyer, part of Quicken Suite 2000, can help. The program walks you through a simple interview process, and then generates a document based on the laws of your state. As you go through the interview, Quicken Family Lawyer always provides plain-English explanations and help so the legalese doesn't confuse you.

Setting Up Quicken Family Lawyer

Quicken Family Lawyer comes as a separate CD-ROM in the Quicken Suite 2000 package.

To install Quicken Family Lawyer:

1. Insert the Family Lawyer CD-ROM into your CD-ROM drive. Windows should automatically begin the installation. If it doesn't (not an uncommon occurrence), try ejecting and reinserting the CD-ROM. If that still doesn't work, choose Start > Settings > Control Panel, then double-click Add/Remove Programs (**Figure 21.1**). Click the Install button, insert the Family Lawyer CD-ROM, and follow the onscreen instructions.

2. The Family Lawyer Setup program opens. Follow the onscreen instructions to complete the installation.

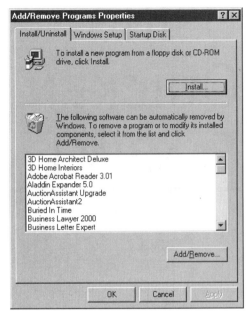

Figure 21.1 If the Family Lawyer installer doesn't run automatically, use the Add/Remove Programs Control Panel.

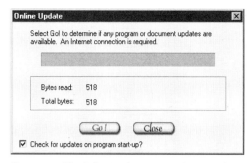

Figure 21.2. The Online Update screen gives you the opportunity to download the latest update of Family Lawyer 2000.

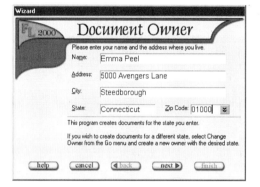

Figure 21.3 The Document Owner Wizard lets you create a personal profile. Fill in your name and mailing address, which most legal documents require, and Quicken Family Lawyer remembers the profile in subsequent visits.

To run Quicken Family Lawyer for the first time:

1. Choose Start > Programs > Quicken > Family Lawyer 2000.

2. Because this is the first time that you've run Quicken Family Lawyer, you'll get the Electronic Registration Card, which you should fill out and either send via your Internet connection or print out and mail the old-fashioned way. You can also click the Register Later button, but the Electronic Registration Card will keep tormenting you every time you start the program until you register.

3. Via your Internet connection, Family Lawyer 2000 has the ability to detect and download program updates. Whenever you start the program, you'll get the Online Update screen, which asks if you want to check for these updates (**Figure 21.2**). Click the Go! button to connect and check. A dialog box will inform you if updates are available. If so, click Yes to download and install the update.

   If you don't want to see the Online Update screen every time you use the program, uncheck the box next to "Check for updates on program start-up?"

4. After you've dealt with the Electronic Registration Card and Online Update, Quicken Family Lawyer opens to the Document Owner Wizard (**Figure 21.3**). Fill in your name and address, and then click Next.

5. This screen asks if you want Quicken Family Lawyer to suggest documents that you should create based on your particular situation. The first time through the program, it's a good idea to click Yes and then click Next. The Document Advisor window appears. Click the Next button.

(continued)

SETTING UP QUICKEN FAMILY LAWYER

6. The next several screens ask if you are familiar with a living trust; your marital status; the name and address of your spouse (if married); and if you have any children. Answer these questions, clicking Next after each one. At the end of the process, the final Document Advisor screen shows you the list of documents that Quicken Family Lawyer recommends you create (**Figure 21.4**). Click the Finish button.

7. The Select User screen appears; if you like, you can click Add to create another user. To create documents for the user you've just created, click OK.

The Documents window appears with a scrolling list of all the documents that Quicken Family Lawyer can create (**Figure 21.5**). The paper clip icon next to a document's name indicates documents that the Document Advisor suggests. On the right side of the window, you'll find a brief explanation of whatever document you've selected in the list, along with suggestions for when you should create such a document and when you should update it.

✔ Tip

■ Above the scrolling list of documents, you'll find a drop-down menu that lets you select specific document types, such as Suggested Document, Powers of Attorney, or Employment. Use this menu to winnow the list to just the kind of document you want.

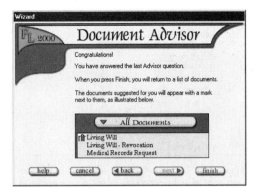

Figure 21.4 When you're done with the Document Advisor, you see a list of recommended documents to create.

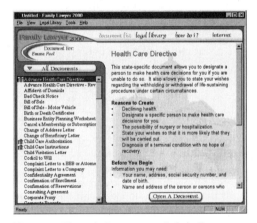

Figure 21.5 The main Documents window allows you to choose any of the 150 legal documents within Quicken Family Lawyer.

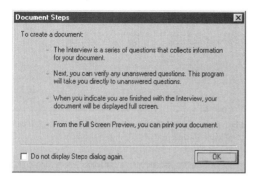

Figure 21.6 The Document Steps dialog box gives you instructions for the Document Interview.

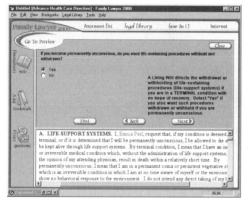

Figure 21.7 The Document Interview is the heart of Quicken Family Lawyer.

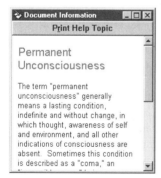

Figure 21.8 Each topic or question in the Document Interview has its own specialized help screen.

Using Quicken Family Lawyer

Once you've entered your basic information, you want to start creating the documents that you need. Quicken Family Lawyer creates customized documents by interviewing you and then plugging your answers into a standardized boilerplate document.

To create a legal document:

1. From the scrolling list in the main Documents screen (refer to **Figure 21.5**), select the name of the document you want to create.

2. Click the "Open A Document" button at the bottom of the screen, or choose File > New. The Document Steps dialog box appears (**Figure 21.6**). Read the instructions in the dialog box, and then click OK. The Document Interview Window appears (**Figure 21.7**).

   The Document Interview window asks questions in the top half of the window and adds your answers to the document that it is creating in the bottom half of the window. So that you can easily see what information you're adding to the document, it appears in red text on your screen (although to assure that the document is legal, it will print in black text regardless of whether you have a color printer).

3. As you finish each question, click Next to proceed to the next question. When you click Next, a help window pops up with a description or definition of the next question's topic (**Figure 21.8**).

   The Document Interview varies in length depending on the particular document that you are creating and the answers that you give.

(continued)

4. When you get to the end of the interview, Family Lawyer alerts you if you've left out any important information (**Figure 21.9**). Click Yes to go back and answer a question with missing information.

5. When you're done, Family Lawyer lets you know (**Figure 21.10**) and gives you the choice of printing the document or previewing it onscreen. If you want to preview the document, click the Next button. Otherwise, to print it, choose File > Print.

✔ Tips

■ Once you add a name and address for anyone, you can access that information for all future documents by choosing it from drop-down lists in the Document Interview window.

■ Choose Help > How Do I? if you're ever unsure how to proceed within Quicken Family Lawyer.

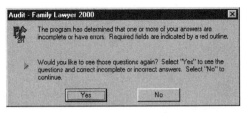

Figure 21.9 Family Lawyer lets you know if you left out vital information in the Document Interview.

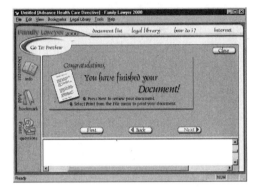

Figure 21.10 In the final Document Interview screen, you have a choice of printing or previewing the document.

Only Part of the Solution

This is a good place for the obligatory caveat: Though attorneys prepared the documents from Quicken Family Lawyer 2000 and checked their legality in all 50 states, Family Lawyer shouldn't replace professional advice. Your particular situation may be complex and require the hands-on assistance of your attorney—especially for documents like wills, where a mistake can have grave consequences. It's a good idea for you to use the document you get from Quicken Family Lawyer 2000 as a starting point, and then have your lawyer review it.

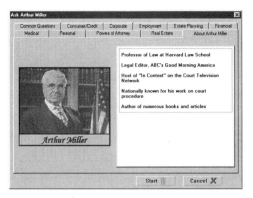

Figure 21.11 You can get answers to some legal questions from a Harvard Law School professor in this window. Pick one of the 10 main legal topic areas to get started.

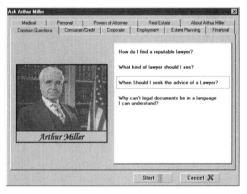

Figure 21.12 In this window you'll find frequently asked questions for each legal topic.

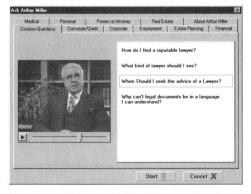

Figure 21.13 When you double-click a question, its answer appears in a video clip next to the question window.

Answering Common Legal Questions

Quicken Family Lawyer includes answers to common legal questions from Arthur Miller, a Harvard Law School professor and author. Miller supplies answers on 10 common legal topics, including estate planning, consumer information, and employment considerations.

To help you puzzle out the meaning of individual legal terms, Quicken Family Lawyer includes a Legal Glossary.

To get answers to legal questions:

1. Choose Legal Library > Ask Arthur Miller. The main Ask Arthur Miller screen appears (**Figure 21.11**).

2. Select a legal topic by clicking its tab. The screen changes to list common questions on that topic (**Figure 21.12**).

3. Double-click a question, and the video window next to the question plays a video clip of Miller answering that question (**Figure 21.13**).

✔ Tip

- You must have more than a 256-color display and have the Family Lawyer 2000 CD in your CD-ROM drive to view the video clips.

To use the Legal Glossary:

1. Choose Legal Library > Glossary. The Glossary screen appears (**Figure 21.14**).

2. Click on the letter that the term you're looking for begins with, and then scroll the list of terms on the left side of the window until you find your term.

3. Click on the term to select it, and the definition appears in the list on the right side of the window.

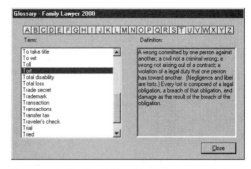

Figure 21.14 The Legal Glossary gives you succinct definitions of legal terms.

Documents in Quicken Family Lawyer 2000

Estate Planning and Administration

- Affidavit of Domicile
- Change of Beneficiary Letter
- Codicil to Will
- Eight varieties of Wills
- Employee Death Benefits Letter
- Estate Planning Worksheets
- Estate Size Worksheets with Tax Calculators
- Exhibit
- Five kinds of Living Trusts
- Five Power of Attorney documents
- Life Insurance Proceeds Letter
- Memorial Plans
- Personal Fact Sheet
- Pour-Over Will
- Social Security Earnings and Benefits Letter
- Stock Power
- Survivor Checklist
- Two Trust Letters to banks or mortgage lenders
- Veteran Benefits Request for Information

Health and Medical

- Advance Health Care Directive
- Advance Health Care Directive—Revocation
- Do-Not-Resuscitate Guide
- Four Medicare letters
- Health Care Power of Attorney
- Health Care Power of Attorney—Revocation
- Insurance Claim Denial Letter
- Living Will
- Living Will—Revocation
- Medical Records Request
- Organ Donation Forms

Family and Personal

- Change of Address letter
- Child Care letters
- Demand for Alimony Payment
- Demand for Child Support Payment
- Divorce Worksheet
- Premarital Agreement
- Request for Birth or Death Certificates
- Request for Marriage or Divorce Documents
- Requests for School Records and Transcripts

Sales, Leases, and Real Estate

- Bill of Sale
- Equipment lease
- Eviction Notice
- Four real estate lease agreements
- General Receipt
- Home Sale Worksheet
- Homeowners' Association Proxy
- Intent to Purchase Real Estate
- Landlord's Notice to Enter
- Late Rent Notice
- Moving Checklist
- Rental Application
- Renter's Inspection Worksheet
- Security Deposit Refund letter
- Tenant's Notice to Terminate

(continued)

Documents in Quicken Family Lawyer 2000 *(continued)*

Credit and Consumer

- Bad Check notice
- Cancel membership or subscription letter
- Consumer complaint letters
- Credit Card letters
- Credit Report letters
- Demand for Undelivered Product
- Small Claims Worksheet
- Stop Payment on Check letter

Business and Employment

- Confidentiality Agreement
- Consulting Agreement
- Corporate Minutes form
- Corporate Proxy
- Corporate records worksheet
- Employment Resignation letter
- Five employment agreements
- Four types of promissory note
- License Agreement
- Non-Compete Agreement
- Notice of Meeting
- Unanimous Consent form
- Waiver of Notice form
- Work for Hire Agreement

Government Letters and Forms

- Letter to Government Official
- Response to IRS Notice
- Response to IRS Penalty
- Form 1310—Claim Refund Due Deceased Taxpayer
- Form 2848—Power of Attorney
- Form 4506—Request for Copy of Tax Form
- Form 8332—Release of Claim to Exemption
- Form 8822—Change of Address
- Form SS-4—Application for Employer ID Number
- Form W-10—Dependent Care Provider's ID
- Form W-4—Withholding Allowance Certificate
- Form W-5—Advanced Earned Income Credit
- Form W-9—Request for Taxpayer ID Number

PART 4

RUNNING A
SMALL BUSINESS

Setting Up Your Small Business

Many small businesses begin in the home, growing out of hobbies, secret passions, or the simple desire to be your own boss. At one time or another, most people have thought about starting a business of their own. But if you do start your own business, having tight control over your finances is a must.

Quicken already did a great job of handling home finances. By adding invoicing, customer statements, and simple accounts payable and accounts receivable to Quicken Deluxe, Intuit created Quicken Home & Business to serve the legions of budding entrepreneurs.

In order to set up Quicken Home & Business, you'll need to create a few business accounts; make sure that you have categories that match your business; and tell the program a little about the products or services that you sell.

Creating Business Accounts

One of your first decisions in setting up your business is to figure out the division of your bank accounts. Will you create a separate checking account for your business, or will you run your business out of your personal checking account? I strongly recommend that you create a separate checking account for the business, and that you use that account for as many of your business transactions as you can. It makes things cleaner and easier when you're doing your bills, at tax time, and if the Internal Revenue Service ever audits you (something I hope never happens).

Because most businesses are designed to make money, you'll need to set up an account for money that customers owe you, called Accounts Receivable. In Quicken Home & Business, you handle accounts receivable by invoicing your clients. So you'll set up an Invoices/Receivables account within Quicken.

Your business will also spend money on various bills. Money going out of your business is called Accounts Payable, and the corresponding account type within Quicken Home & Business is a Bills/Payables account.

Is It Right for Your Business?

Quicken Home & Business, with its ability to handle invoicing, payables, and receivables, can meet the needs of many small businesses, but review it carefully to make sure that it will work for yours.

Intuit designed Quicken Home & Business for home-based businesses with fewer than four employees, run by an entrepreneur who would rather handle home and work finances together than use a separate accounting program for the business.

Perhaps the best way to see whether the program is a good match for your business is to list the things Quicken Home & Business doesn't do. If these are features you need, you should consider a full accounting package, such as Intuit's QuickBooks or QuickBooks Pro.

Quicken Home & Business doesn't handle payroll (although the CD-ROM includes a trial version of QuickPayroll, which is a subscription-based system for small business payrolls), inventory tracking, or purchase orders. It can't apply finance charges automatically to invoices. It's not a multiuser program. It doesn't do double entry bookkeeping, and there's no audit trail. Finally, you won't find such niceties as estimates, job costing, or time tracking.

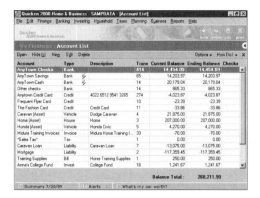

Figure 22.1 As with all new accounts, your business accounts get started in the Account List.

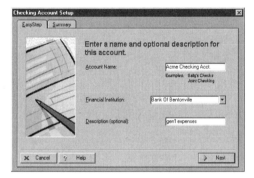

Figure 22.2 Enter the name and description of your business checking account.

To create the business checking account:

1. You create a business checking account in the same way that you create a personal checking account. There is a detailed rundown of the process in Chapter 2; refer to that chapter if you need step-by-step help. Briefly, choose Finance > Account List. The Account List appears.

2. At the top of the Account List (**Figure 22.1**), click New. The Create New Account window appears. Choose Checking, then click Next.

3. The Checking Account Setup window appears (**Figure 22.2**). Enter the business checking account name, the financial institution, and a brief (and optional) description.

4. Follow the rest of the EasyStep directions to set up the account.

To create the Invoices/Receivables and Bills/Payables accounts:

1. Choose Finance > Account List, or press [Ctrl][A] to open the Account List.

2. At the top of the Account List, click the New button. The Create New Account window appears (**Figure 22.3**).

3. Click either the Invoices/Receivables button or the Bills/Payables button, then click Next.

4. In the next screen (**Figure 22.4**), enter the name and an optional description of the account you are creating, then click Next.

5. You'll see a help screen explaining what to do with your new account. Click Next.

6. The Summary screen lets you change your entries if necessary. Click Done when you're through.

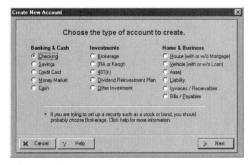

Figure 22.3 Choose either the Invoices/Receivables button or the Bills/Payables button.

Figure 22.4 Give your Invoices/Receivables or Bills/Payables account a name, and you're done.

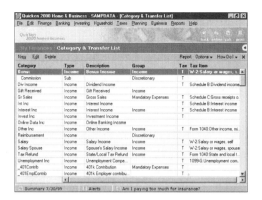

Figure 22.5 To delete or add categories, start with the Category & Transfer List.

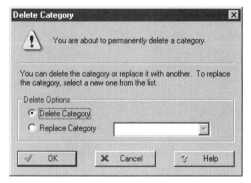

Figure 22.6 In this dialog box, you can either delete a category altogether, or assign its transactions to another category.

Checking Your Categories

When you installed Quicken Home & Business, the preset list of categories included both personal and business categories. These categories, though fairly complete, are naturally somewhat generic. You'll need to go through the Category and Transfer List to weed out categories that you don't need and (less likely) add any categories specific to your business.

To delete unneeded categories:

1. Choose Finance > Category & Transfer List. The Category & Transfer List appears (**Figure 22.5**).

2. Scroll through the list until you find a category that you would like to delete. Click once on the category to select it, then click the Delete button at the top of the Category & Transfer List. The Delete Category dialog box appears (**Figure 22.6**).

3. You have a choice of deleting the category or replacing it with another category. When you replace a category, Quicken deletes the category from the category list and replaces it in the category field of any transactions with the new category you've selected. Make your choice, then click OK.

✔ Tip

- It's no big deal to delete a category you've never used for a transaction, but if you have, deleting the category removes it from the category list and erases it from the Category field of any transactions to which you've it. If you delete a subcategory, Quicken deletes it from the category list and reassigns its transactions to the parent category.

To add new categories:

◆ Follow the directions in Chapter 3 under "To create a new category or subcategory."

Entering Your Products and Services

With Quicken Home & Business, you can create and send invoices, billing your customers for the products and services that you supply. Invoices contain line items, listing the individual products and services, and their prices. Rather than entering your products or services individually on each invoice, you can enter them just once and access them from drop-down lists when you fill out an invoice.

To enter a product or service:

1. Choose Customize > Business > Invoice Items. The Customize Invoice Items window appears (**Figure 22.7**).

2. Click New. The New Item window appears (**Figure 22.8**).

3. Enter the item name, or if you prefer, an item number.

4. From the drop-down list, choose a category for the item.

5. Enter a description of the item (optional).

6. The line item can, if you want, be a subtotal of the preceding items. See the sidebar "Subtotal and Percentage Items" for more detail.

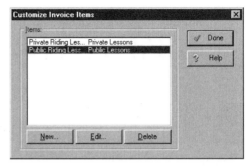

Figure 22.7 Quicken can store invoice items so you don't need to type them on every invoice.

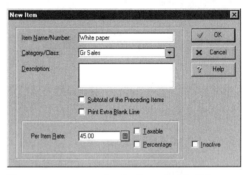

Figure 22.8 Enter new invoice items in this dialog box.

7. The Print Extra Blank Line check box adds a blank line after any subtotal item.

8. Enter the Per Item Rate. This can be the amount that you charge per hour for a service or it can be a flat rate for a product.

9. If you charge sales tax for this item, click the Taxable check box.

10. You can use a Percentage item to have Quicken calculate a customer discount or surcharge. See the sidebar "Subtotal and Percentage Items" for more information.

11. When you're done adding the New Item, click the OK button.

Subtotal and Percentage Items

On invoices, you'll often want to subtotal some line items, then get a grand total on the bottom line of the invoice. For example, you might be working on two different projects for the same client, but you prefer to send her one invoice. You could enter all the line items for the first project, insert a subtotal line so that the client knows how much that project cost, then continue with the line items for the second project, adding a second subtotal at the end. When you insert a subtotal line, Quicken adds up all of the line items above, up to the previous subtotal.

You must use a subtotal if you want to use a Percentage item to apply a customer discount or surcharge. Quicken calculates the percentage on the line immediately preceding the Percentage line, so if you want to apply a discount to a number of line items, you'll need to subtotal them first, then apply the Percentage to the subtotal. To apply the Percentage, enter a negative number for a discount, or use a positive number for a surcharge in the Per Item Rate field.

ENTERING YOUR PRODUCTS AND SERVICES

INVOICING & RECEIVING BUSINESS INCOME

As the owner of a small business myself, I can attest that it's awfully satisfying to send out an invoice, receive the payment, and deposit the check. And that's basically the process you need to take with your business as you make sales and receive income.

You begin by making the sale and creating an invoice in Quicken Home & Business for your product or service. After some reasonable interval, your client sends a check in payment. You apply that payment to the invoice in Quicken. If the payment isn't enough to cover the entire amount, Quicken lets you know how much the customer still owes. If you need to, you can print customer statements that keep track of ongoing invoices and summarize both received and outstanding payments.

In the event that you actually have to give money back to one of your clients, you can issue a credit, or even cut a refund check right from the Accounts Receivable register.

Creating and Printing Invoices

You create invoices from the Invoices/Receivables account register. If you haven't already created this account, see Chapter 22 for detailed instructions.

To create and print an invoice:

1. Choose Business > Create Invoice. If you have more than one Invoice account and none of the registers is open, the Choose Invoice Account dialog opens (**Figure 23.1**). Choose an account from the pull-down and click OK. The account register opens with a blank invoice on top (**Figure 23.2**).

2. From the Create New tools menu at the top of the register (**Figure 23.3**), scroll down and choose Invoice.

3. In the Customer field, enter the customer's name. QuickFill memorizes the name automatically so that next time you can choose it from the drop-down list.

4. The Template field lets you choose from invoice templates that you can create and customize. There's more about customizing invoices later in this chapter; for now, use the Invoice Default template.

5. QuickFill has already placed the customer name in the Bill To field; now enter the rest of the customer's address. QuickFill remembers that for future use, too.

6. You can instantly copy the name and address information from the Bill To field into the Ship To field by pressing the single-quote key (`'`). You can also leave the Ship To field blank.

7. Quicken inserts today's date as the invoice date automatically, but you can change it if you want.

Figure 23.1 The Choose Invoice Account dialog opens so you can assign your billing to the right account.

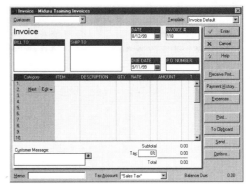

Figure 23.2 The blank invoice is ready to be filled in with the aid of QuickFill.

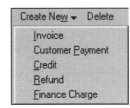

Figure 23.3 The Create New menu lets you create invoices, payments, credits, refunds, or finance charges.

Figure 23.4 Change the automatic due date for invoices in the Invoice Options window.

Figure 23.5 Pick an invoice item from the drop-down list.

8. Enter an invoice number under Invoice #. It can be any number that you want, and Quicken will increment future invoice numbers by one.

9. Quicken calculates the Due Date based on the invoice options. You can enter another date here, or click the Options button on the invoice form. The Invoice Options window appears (**Figure 23.4**). If you prefer, change the Default Due Date, then click OK.

10. If the customer has given you a purchase order number, enter it in the P.O. Number field.

11. Now you'll begin entering line items in the invoice. The first field is Category, which is an income category. You can enter a new category here, but you probably won't have to, because this field will fill in automatically when you enter Item (the next field).

12. In the Item field, select an invoice item from the drop-down list (**Figure 23.5**). If the item that you want isn't in the list, you can click the New button at the bottom of the drop-down list to create a new item on the spot. When you select an item, the Category field automatically fills in.

13. The Description field may or may not have an entry already, depending on how you set up the invoice item. If you like, you can add a detailed description of the line item.

14. Enter a number in the Qty field. If you're selling services for which you charge by the hour, enter the number of hours. If you're selling goods, enter the number of units the customer is buying.

(continued)

CREATING AND PRINTING INVOICES

15. In the Rate field, enter the unit price for goods or the hourly price for services.

16. Quicken calculates the line item Amount by multiplying the Qty by the Rate.

17. To charge sales tax for the line item, press the ⊤ key in the Tax field. If you set up the invoice item as taxable in Invoice Items (see Chapter 22), this happened automatically.

18. Repeat steps 11 to 17 for as many line items as you have.

19. You can optionally enter anything you like (up to 50 characters) in the Customer Message field. This message prints in the lower left corner of the invoice.

20. The Memo is also optional; it's for your information only and doesn't print on the invoice.

21. The Tax Account field shows what liability account the sales taxes you charge will go to. The first time you create an invoice, Quicken creates a Sales Tax liability account. The sales tax percentage that you enter on this first invoice will be associated with the Sales Tax liability account in the future. If you sell items at different tax rates, you must set up additional accounts, one for each rate. You can then choose any of the Sales Tax liability accounts from the Tax Account drop-down list.

22. Congratulations—you've filled out your invoice (**Figure 23.6**).

Figure 23.6 The completed invoice, ready for you to save or print.

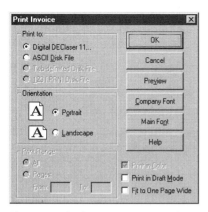

Figure 23.7 Check your print settings, then click OK to print your invoice.

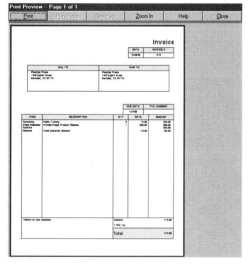

Figure 23.8 You can see what your invoice will look like on paper in the Print Preview window.

Form button

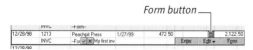

Figure 23.9 Click the Form button to open an invoice for editing from the register.

23. To save the invoice, click the Enter button. To print the invoice, click Print. The Print Invoice window appears (**Figure 23.7**). Check the settings, then click OK. If you want to see how the invoice will print before committing it to paper, click the Preview button to open the Print Preview window (**Figure 23.8**). If the invoice looks okay, click the Print button in this window. Otherwise, click Close and modify the invoice.

You can also save the invoice to the Clipboard by clicking the button with that name, or you can send it via e-mail by clicking the Send button.

To edit a saved invoice:

1. In the Invoices account register, select the invoice you want to change.

2. Click the Form button (**Figure 23.9**). The invoice form opens, and you can make changes as needed.

3. When you're done editing, click the Enter button.

✔ Tips

■ The Due Date field must contain a date, but you can still enter a payment instruction, such as "Payment due upon receipt," by typing it in the Customer Message field.

■ If you sell services at a flat rate, you can leave the Qty and Rate fields blank, and simply enter the fee in the Amount field.

Customizing Invoices

Quicken comes with default invoice and credit memo forms, which you can use as is or customize for your business. Most people will want to customize the existing forms or create entirely new ones from scratch. You can have as many invoice and credit memo forms as you like to cover different aspects of your business. For example, you can have one sort of invoice for taxable items and another for nontaxable products.

Quicken Home & Business doesn't give you a complete invoice editor; instead, you can show, hide, and rename fields, and add a graphic for your company logo. That's usually enough for most small businesses. If you need more control over the look of your invoices, you should look into getting preprinted forms or consider using Intuit's QuickBooks, which has more facilities for designing invoices.

To create or customize an invoice form:

1. Open the Invoices register.

2. From the Create New menu, choose Invoice. A blank invoice form appears.

3. In the form, choose Edit from the bottom of the Template drop-down list. The Customize Templates window appears (**Figure 23.10**).

4. To create a new template, click New. To edit an existing template, select it in the Customize Templates window and click Edit. Depending on which button you click, the New Template or Edit Template window appears (**Figure 23.11**).

Figure 23.10 Begin editing form templates in the Customize Templates window.

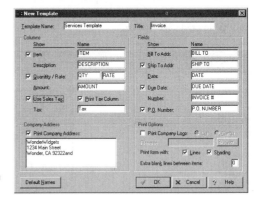

Figure 23.11 The New Template and Edit Template windows are virtually identical. Either one lets you change forms. This is the New Template window.

5. Enter the Template Name and Title. The Template Name is what appears in the Template drop-down list, and the Title prints at the top of the form.

6. In the Columns area, you must fill in the Description and Amount fields. The other fields are optional. You can change the name of any column by entering a new name in the text field. To have a column appear on the form, make sure that you've selected the checkbox next to it.

7. In the Fields area, you must include Bill To Addr, Date, and Number. The other fields are optional. You can change the name of any field by entering a new name. To have a field appear on the form, make sure that you've selected the checkbox next to it.

8. If you want to include your Company Address, click the Print Company Address checkbox and enter the address in the field below.

9. Under Print Options, you can add a bitmapped logo (created in Paintbrush or other graphics program) by clicking the checkbox next to Print Company Logo, then clicking the Browse button and browsing to the graphics file. The file must have a .bmp file extension. You can also click the Center radio button to center the logo on the page, or the Left button to put the logo to the left of your company address.

10. Click OK to save the template changes, then click Done in the Manage Templates window.

Receiving Customer Payments

Ah, here's the good part. You've pulled a payment check out of your mailbox, and you need to enter it into Quicken. Rather than simply entering it as a deposit in your business checking account, you'll enter the customer payment in your Invoices/Receivables register, applying the payment against an outstanding invoice.

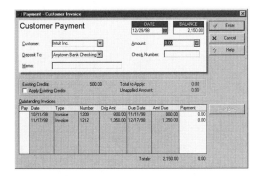

Figure 23.12 You'll use the Payment window to apply customer payments to outstanding invoices.

To receive a customer payment:

1. Open the Invoices register.

2. From the Create New menu, choose Customer Payment. A Payment window appears (**Figure 23.12**).

3. Choose the Customer from the drop-down list. When you do, the customer's balance and outstanding invoice history appear in the window.

4. Enter the amount of the check and the check number.

5. From the Deposit To drop-down list, choose the checking account that will receive the funds (usually your business checking account).

6. Add a memo about the payment (optional).

7. If the customer has existing credits, as does the one in Figure 23.12, you'll see that amount in the Existing Credits area. To add the credit to the amount of the payment that you have received, click the Apply Existing Credits checkbox.

8. Quicken automatically applies the payment (plus existing credits, if any) to the oldest invoice for that customer. Quicken shows which invoice it is applying payment to by putting a green checkmark next to the invoice. If that's the invoice for which the customer has sent payment, you can leave the checkmark as it is. Otherwise, click the checkmark next to the proper invoice. You can split a payment over multiple invoices by selecting each invoice and entering the amount you are applying in the Payment column.

9. Click Enter to save your work. Quicken records the payment in the Invoices register and makes a deposit entry in your checking account.

RECEIVING CUSTOMER PAYMENTS

Entering Credits and Refunds

This part isn't nearly as much fun as receiving payments. Sometimes you need to issue credits to your customers, and other times you actually need to refund money.

You issue credits for a variety of reasons. A customer may prepay an invoice or give you money as a retainer. Or the customer may return a product for credit on future invoices.

When you issue a refund, you cut a check for the amount of a refund and send it to the customer. You might need to do this because the customer has returned a product with extreme dissatisfaction, and wants money back instead of a credit.

To enter a credit:

1. Open the Invoices register.

2. From the Create New menu, choose Credit. The Credit—Customer Invoice window appears (**Figure 23.13**).

3. You enter a credit in much the same way you would enter an invoice. Choose a customer from the Customer drop-down list, then enter a line item for the amount of the credit.

4. When you're done entering line items, click Print to print the credit memo, then click Enter to save your work.

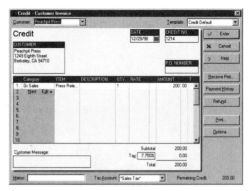

Figure 23.13 Credit memos work like invoices—but in reverse.

Figure 23.14 Painful as they may be, refunds are easy to generate with Quicken Home & Business.

To enter a refund:

1. Open the Invoices register.

2. From the Create New menu, choose Refund. The Refund—Customer Invoice window appears (**Figure 23.14**).

3. Choose a checking account from the Account to Pay From drop-down list, and choose Print Check from the Type of Transaction drop-down list. Fill out the Customer and Amount information, then click Enter.

ENTERING CREDITS AND REFUNDS

Printing Customer Statements

A customer statement is a report that summarizes a customer's account. It includes invoices, credit memos, and payments that you've received and applied. At the bottom, it shows the aging (how many days overdue) of the invoices.

To print a customer statement:

1. Choose Business > Create Statement. The Customer Statements window appears (**Figure 23.15**).

2. From the Template drop-down list, choose a statement template. You can customize customer statements as you would invoices and credit memos.

3. In the Customers area, choose All, Selected, or just one customer.

4. Enter the date range for the statement.

5. Click the appropriate checkbox if you don't want to print statements with a zero balance.

6. Click Print.

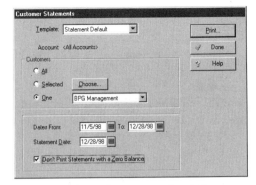

Figure 23.15 Choose the customers for which you want to print statements from this window.

RECORDING AND PAYING BUSINESS BILLS

RECORDING AND PAYING BUSINESS BILLS

It costs money to run a business, and paying bills is an important—though not especially fun—part of your business operations. Just as in the rest of the program, you'll use an account to track your business bills—in this case, the Bills/Payables liability account that you should have created in Chapter 22. If you haven't already created your account, this is a good time to turn to Chapter 22.

The best way to handle bills using Quicken Home & Business is to enter a bill in the Bills/Payables account register, then immediately schedule a payment. Quicken will remind you when to pay the bill, keeping you from getting behind. You'll also use the Bills/Payables register to record any credits or refunds that you receive from your vendors.

Entering Bills and Scheduling Payments

You get the maximum benefit from Quicken Home & Business if you enter a bill, then schedule payment for it. Quicken can show you a running total of your Accounts Payable, and automatically reminds you to make the payments as they come due.

To enter a bill and schedule payment:

1. Choose Business > Create Bill. If you have more than one Invoice account and none of the registers is open, the Choose Invoice Account dialog opens (**Figure 24.1**). Choose an account from the pull-down menu and click OK. The account register opens with a blank bill on top (**Figure 24.2**).

   From an open Bills register, you can select Create New from the tools at the top of the register (**Figure 24.3**) and scroll down to Bill.

2. Choose a name from the drop-down Vendor list, or if it's a new vendor you're paying, enter the name in the Vendor field.

3. Enter the Vendor Address (optional).

4. Quicken fills in the Date and Due Date fields for you, but you can change them if you want.

5. Enter the Bill No. and the P.O. Number (optional).

6. In the line items area, select an expense category from the drop-down Category list. You can add a new expense category by entering its name and pressing (Enter). Quicken asks if you want to create a new category; click Yes, then fill out the Set Up Category window.

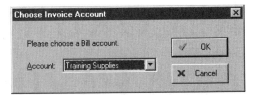

Figure 24.1 Select the account from which you want to pay the bill from the pull-down list.

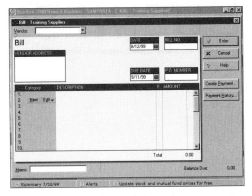

Figure 24.2 Use this form to help track your accounts payable.

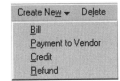

Figure 24.3 From the register, scroll down the Create New list to Bill.

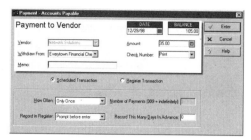

Figure 24.4 It's best to schedule payment as soon as you enter the bill.

7. Enter a description of the item in the Description field (optional).

8. The E column is for reimbursable expenses that you can add to a customer invoice (optional).

9. Enter the amount of the bill in the Amount field.

10. To save the bill and enter payments later, click Enter. Otherwise, click Create Payment to set up a new scheduled transaction. The Payment window appears (**Figure 24.4**).

11. Quicken fills in the Date, Balance, and Vendor fields for you, but you may change them if you want. In fact, you'll probably want to change the Date field to reflect a future payment date.

12. Enter the amount of the scheduled payment in the Amount field.

13. Choose the checking account to use from the Withdraw From drop-down list.

14. From the Check Number drop-down list, choose Print (if you print your checks from within Quicken) or Next Check Number (if you write your checks by hand).

15. Click the Scheduled Transaction radio button.

16. Use the drop-down lists to set the number and frequency of the scheduled payments and to tell Quicken whether to remind you or enter them automatically in your register.

17. Click Enter to save the scheduled transaction.

To view the payment history:

1. In the Bills/Payables register, select the bill for which you want to see the payment history, then click the Form button. The Bill form appears.

2. Click the Payment History button. The Payment History window appears (**Figure 24.5**).

3. Click Done.

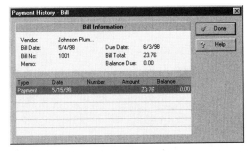

Figure 24.5 The Payment History window shows you all of the payments applied to the selected bill.

Do You Need To Use Accounts Payable?

If you always pay your business bills when you receive them rather than waiting until they are due, there is no need to set up the Bills/Payables account and use the Accounts Payable features in Quicken Home & Business. Instead, track bills in Quicken by entering the bill as a check (postdated, if you prefer) in your business checking account register, or in the Write Checks window.

If you prefer to hold off on paying bills until their due date, then it makes more sense to set up a Bills/Payables account.

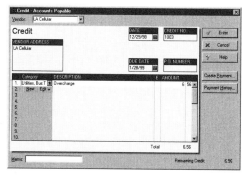

Figure 24.6 The Credit window lets you create vendor credits that you can later apply to their bills.

Figure 24.7 Fill out the Refund window to record a refund that you receive from a vendor.

Handling Vendor Credits and Refunds

On occasion, one of your vendors will issue you a credit or a refund. It could be because you returned a defective product or because the vendor accidentally overcharged you. Either way, you need to enter it as a credit against your Accounts Payable. A Credit form looks and works a lot like a Bill form.

To enter vendor credits:

1. In your Bills/Payables register, choose Create New > Credit. A Credit window appears (**Figure 24.6**).

2. Fill out the Credit window in the same way that you filled out the Bill window in the section above. Enter information in the Vendor, Date, and Due Date fields, and enter the line items for the credit.

3. Click Enter. Quicken enters the credit in the register, reducing the amount that you owe the vendor. This creates an existing credit that you can apply the next time you pay a bill to this vendor.

To enter vendor refunds:

1. In your Bills/Payables register, choose Create New > Refund. A Refund window appears (**Figure 24.7**).

2. Select the destination checking account from the Account to Deposit To dropdown list.

3. Enter the Vendor, Date, and Amount of the transaction.

4. Click Enter to save your work.

GETTING
BUSINESS REPORTS

Reports are vital to running your business well. You'll use reports to see which customers owe you money, what bills you need to pay, and how healthy your business is.

You will also want to run reports that let your accountant know the status of your business. And when it comes time to file your business tax return, reports can tell you which of your expenses are tax deductible.

About Business Reports

You create business reports in Quicken Home & Business in much the same way that you create reports for your personal income and expenditures—by choosing Reports > Business > [name of report] (**Figure 25.1**). You can also operate out of the Reports and Graphs Center, where each report type is accompanied by a sample.

For detailed instructions on how to create and customize reports, turn to Chapter 17. Rather than repeat those instructions below, I'll explain the different types of business reports.

Profit & Loss statements

A Profit & Loss statement for your business is similar to an income and expense report that you'd create for your personal finances. The statement includes income and expenses by category (**Figure 25.2**). Your business income and expenses are totaled at the bottom of the report; if the number is positive, your business has made a profit. A negative number, of course, shows that your business lost money during the time period of the report.

You can also create a Profit & Loss Comparison Report that shows side-by-side columns comparing figures for two periods—for example Year to Date and Month to Date, or Current Quarter and Last Quarter.

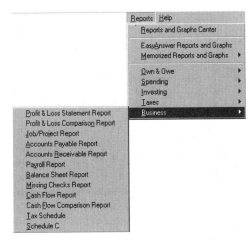

Figure 25.1 The pull-down list shows the types of reports you can generate for your business.

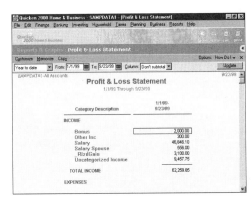

Figure 25.2 Monitor the current financial health of your business with a Profit & Loss statement.

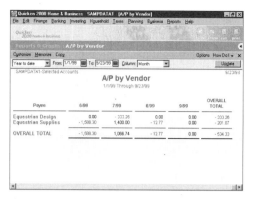

Figure 25.3 Prompt payment will gladden the hearts of your vendors, and the Accounts Payable by Vendor report tells you who needs a check from you.

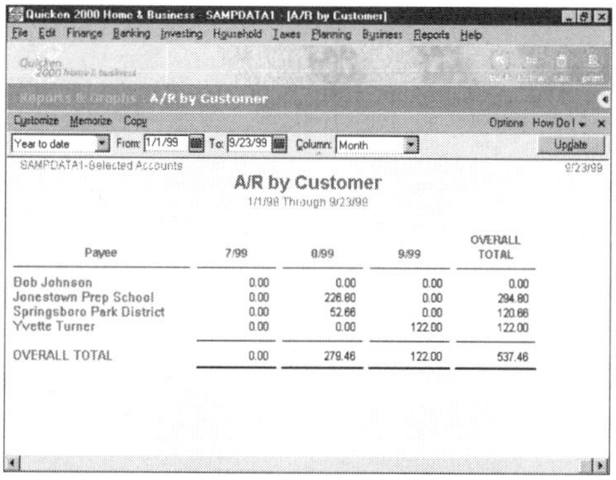

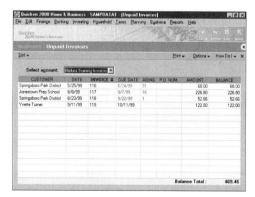

Figure 25.4 Income is imperative to a small business, so track your income often with the Accounts Receivable report.

Figure 25.5 The Unpaid Invoices report shows you how overdue various customers' invoices are, and lets you know which clients need a reminder to pay.

Job/Project reports

Quicken lets you create a report that breaks down your income and expenditures according to project if you have set up each project as a Class. (See Chapter 3 for a discussion of Categories and Classes.) The default report lays out the categories in rows and the classes as columns—but, as with all Quicken's reports, you can customize it to suit your own preferences. You can also set up a Job/Project report to view a comparison of your expenditures during two time periods.

Accounts Payable reports

You'll use Accounts Payable reports to track the amount you owe each vendor and due dates for payment to that vendor is. To create Accounts Payable reports, you'll need to set up a Bills and Payables account, record bills in that account, and schedule payments. To see what you owe, you can create an Accounts Payable by Vendor report (**Figure 25.3**). See Chapter 24 for detailed information about using Accounts Payable.

Accounts Receivable reports

Accounts Receivable reports show you the money that your customers owe you in outstanding invoices and the payment history for invoices (**Figure 25.4**). These reports shouldn't be confused with the Unpaid Invoices report, which shows you invoice aging—or how many days past due an invoice is (**Figure 25.5**). You display the Unpaid Invoices report by choosing Business > Unpaid Invoices. See Chapter 23 for more information about Accounts Receivable reports.

Balance Sheets

Unlike Profit & Loss statements, which focus on the cash flowing in and out of your business, the Balance Sheet takes a wider view of your business's financial health. A Balance Sheet summarizes the overall financial position of your business (**Figure 25.6**). It shows the value of your company's assets, liabilities, and equity as of the date of the report. The reason it's called a balance sheet is because the value of the assets always equals the combined value of the liabilities and equity— that is, they balance.

What is *equity*? Equity is to your business what net worth is to your personal finances. Quicken calculates equity by taking the current year's profit or loss, adding it to the previous year's profit or loss, and adding that amount to the capital you originally invested in the business.

Missing Check reports

When your register just won't balance, or when it seems there's just more money in your account than there ought to be, running a Missing Check report may help pinpoint the problem.

Cash Flow reports

Cash Flow reports can be set up either for a single period or as Cash Flow Comparison reports that show the amounts spent under each category. As always, the usefulness of these reports depends on the accuracy of the data you enter at the front end.

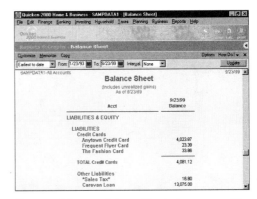

Figure 25.6 Create a Balance Sheet when you need to know your overall financial position.

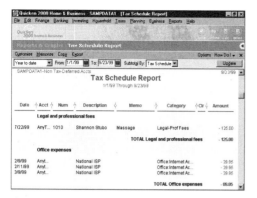

Figure 25.7 The Tax Schedule report includes all tax-related transactions, assigned to the appropriate tax forms.

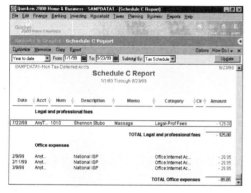

Figure 25.8 The Schedule C report includes just those transactions that you need to report to the IRS using Schedule C.

Tax reports

Most people running a small business report tax-related transactions to the Internal Revenue Service using the Schedule C tax form. If your business is incorporated, you'll need to use forms other than Schedule C; consult your accountant to see which ones. Quicken Home & Business lets you create a Tax Schedule report, which shows you all tax-related transactions assigned to different tax forms (**Figure 25.7**). It also provides a separate Schedule C report, which shows only Schedule C transactions (**Figure 25.8**).

To get good information in either kind of report, you must have Quicken's Tax Links set up correctly. If you need more help in assigning categories to tax forms, see "Linking Categories to Federal Tax Forms" in Chapter 13.

ABOUT BUSINESS REPORTS

INDEX

A

"About this account" window, 141
Account List, 21, 119, 231, 232
account registers. *See* registers
accounts. *See also individual accounts*
    for assets, 138
    balancing, 95–102
    creating with EasyStep, 19–20
    deleting, 22
    description of, 17
    editing, 21
    enabling for online use, 105–107
    excluding from reports, 174
    hiding *vs.* deleting, 22
    maximum number of, 17
    printing list of, 179
    registers for, 31–51
    setting up, 17–22
    transferring money between, 45–47
    types of, 18
    viewing, 21
Accounts center, 84
Accounts menu, 51
Accounts Payable. *See* Bills/Payables account
Accounts Receivable. *See* Invoices/Receivables
    account
Accounts tab, 174, 185
Acrobat Reader, tax forms and, 213
Action Plan screen, 151
Activity Centers, 87–88
Add Pension screen, 195
Add Salary dialog box, 194
addresses, 67
Adjust button, 102
Advanced tab, 174
Alerts & Reminders, 84
Alerts box, 120
Alerts button, 12
alignment, check printing, 68, 69

amortized loans, 121
Ask Arthur Miller screen, 223
asset accounts, 18, 138
assets, 18, 258
Assign Transactions to Group window, 80
ATM withdrawals, 35, 110
automatic operations. *See also* QuickFill feature
    entering check numbers, 34
    saving work, 15
    updating of QuickFill list, 54

B

Back button, 10
backing up data file, 7, 15
Balance Sheets, 258
balances
    adjusting, 102
    entering open balances, 20
    problems with, 97, 98, 100–102
balancing accounts, 95–102
    adjusting ending balance, 102
    checking accounts, 96–98
    correcting transaction errors, 97, 98, 100–102
    credit card accounts, 99
    help topics for, 98
    money market accounts, 96–98
    report for, 98
    savings accounts, 96–98
balloon payments, 122
bank accounts, 18, 138, 230
Banking Center, 87
Banking menu, 9
banking online, 103–113
bar graphs, 184
Billminder, 73, 82
bills
    business, 249, 250–252
    paying online, 103, 111–113
    personal, 103, 111–113
Bills/Payables account, 230, 232, 247–253

INDEX